UNDERSTANDING
THE CATECHISM
Creed

MICHAEL PENNOCK

RESOURCES FOR CHRISTIAN LIVING™
Allen, Texas

"The Ad Hoc Committee to Oversee
the Use of the Catechism,
National Conference of Catholic Bishops,
has found this catechetical series
to be in conformity with
the *Catechism of the Catholic Church*."

President: Kim Duty
Publisher: Maryann Nead
Catechetical Advisor: Jacquie Jambor
Editorial Director: Ed DeStefano

Author: Michael Pennock

Product Manager: Mike Carotta
Project Editor: Karen Griffith
Senior Production Editor: Laura Fremder

Art Director: Pat Bracken
Page Design: Dennis Davidson
Production Manager: Jenna Nelson
Cover Design: Pat Bracken

NIHIL OBSTAT
Rev. Msgr. Glenn D. Gardner, J.C.D.
Censor Librorum

IMPRIMATUR
† Most Rev. Charles V. Grahmann
Bishop of Dallas

March 9, 1998

The Nihil Obstat and Imprimatur are official declarations
that the material reviewed is free of doctrinal or moral
error. No implication is contained therein that those
granting the Nihil Obstat and Imprimatur agree with
the contents, opinions, or statements expressed.

Printed in the United States of America

20250   ISBN 0-7829-0872-1 (Student Book)
20251   ISBN 0-7829-0873-X (Teacher's Guide)

2 3 4 5 6   03 02 01 00 99

ACKNOWLEDGMENTS

Scripture excerpts are taken from the *New American
Bible with Revised New Testament and Psalms*
Copyright © 1991, 1986, 1970 Confraternity of
Christian Doctrine, Washington, DC. Used with permis-
sion. All rights reserved. No part of the *New American
Bible* may be reproduced by any means without the
permission of the copyright owner.

Excerpt from the English translation of the *Catechism
of the Catholic Church* for the United States of America
copyright © 1994 United States Catholic Conference,
Inc.—Libreria Editrice Vaticana. Used with permission.

Excerpts from *Vatican Council II: The Conciliar and
Post Conciliar Documents, New Revised Edition,* Austin
Flannery, O.P., Gen. Ed. Copyright © 1975, 1986, 1992,
1996 by Costello Publishing Company, Inc. Used by
permission.

Photos: Bruce Ayers/Tony Stone Images, 89; Patricia
A. Classick, 30–31; Caspar David Friedrich/SuperStock,
42–43; Full Photographics, 48; Diana Ong/SuperStock,
117; Michael Orton/Tony Stone Images, 6–7; Gene
Plaisted/The Croisers, 97, 104; Josef Polleross/The Stock
Market, 78–79; NASA, 18–19; SuperStock, 47; James J.
Tissot/SuperStock, 32, 54–55, 114–115; © Bill Wittman,
27, 59.

Send all inquiries to:
RCL • Resources for Christian Living™
200 East Bethany Drive
Allen, Texas 75002-3804

Toll Free   800-822-6701
Fax   800-688-8356

Visit us at www.rclweb.com

Contents

Introduction

Welcome to this book on the essential beliefs of our Catholic faith. It derives its inspiration from the *Catechism of the Catholic Church* (CCC), which was published in October 1992. The Catechism presents the essential teachings of our Catholic faith authoritatively, systematically, and comprehensively.

The source of the teachings of our Catholic faith is Sacred Scripture and Sacred Tradition. Both of which pass on to us divine Revelation. Our official church teachers, which we call the Magisterium of the Church, authentically interpret and pass this revelation on to us.

The Catechism is a remarkable resource book for all Catholics. It is divided into four main parts. The four parts have come to be called the four pillars, or foundations, of the Catechism. They are:

❏ The Profession of Faith
  (The Creed)

❏ The Celebration of the Christian Mystery
  (Worship: Liturgy and Sacraments)

❏ Life in Christ
  (Moral Living)

❏ Christian Prayer

The Catechism is more than seven hundred pages in its English translation. As a result, the Catechism itself encourages us to adapt it. This book, *Understanding the Catechism: Creed,* is one part of a four-book series on the Catechism. This series has been especially written for Catholic high school students.

Understanding the Catechism: Creed will introduce you to the major content of the first pillar of the Catechism— "The Profession of Faith." It will introduce you to or review for you the key teachings contained in the Apostles' Creed, one of the ancient professions of faith prayed by the Church.

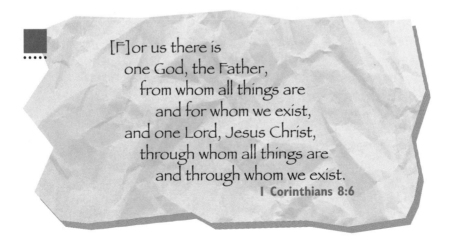

[F]or us there is
one God, the Father,
from whom all things are
and for whom we exist,
and one Lord, Jesus Christ,
through whom all things are
and through whom we exist.
1 Corinthians 8:6

CHAPTER 1

Faith in God

[F]or we walk by faith,
not by sight.
2 CORINTHIANS 5:7

A familiar story tells of a teen out for a walk to get close to nature. While traipsing along a narrow path, he was not watching where he was going. Suddenly he slipped over the edge of a cliff, but luckily he grabbed a branch growing from the side of the cliff. Holding on for dear life but with waning strength, he began desperately calling for help. His plaintive pleas sounded something like this:

Teen: Is anyone up there?
Voice: Yes, I'm here!
Teen: Who are you?
Voice: I'm the Lord.
Teen: Lord, help me!
Voice: Do you trust me?
Teen: I trust you completely, Lord.
Voice: Good. Let go of the branch.
Teen: What?
Voice: I said, "Let go of the branch."
Teen: [After a minute pause] Is anyone else up there?

This young man greatly wanted to be saved, but he lacked one essential ingredient: faith. He was left grasping for dear life to a cragged branch. But over time, either his strength would give out or the branch would break and the teen would be lost.

KEY TERMS

secularism

atheism

agnosticism

secular humanism

hedonism

revelation

salvation history

What difference does having faith in God make in a person's life?

This story is a wonderful parable about people who are seeking happiness and grasping for salvation. Yet so often some people are looking in all the wrong places. The *Catechism of the Catholic Church* comments: "True happiness is not found in riches or well-being, in human fame or power, or in any human achievement—however beneficial it may be—such as science, technology, and art, or indeed in any creature, but in God alone, the source of every good and of all love" (CCC, 1723).

(*Catechism of the Catholic Church,* 1–3, 26–43)

Our Search for Happiness—Our Search for God

Some people do exclude God in their search for happiness. We live in an age filled with **secularism.** Secularism is a view of the world that focuses exclusively on the natural world and holds that the only means of knowing truth is through the natural sciences. We live in a time when many people live without any expressed need for God. Some modern forms of secularism in today's society include:

❏ **Atheism,** which denies that God exists.

❏ **Agnosticism,** which claims that no one can know for sure whether there is a God or not.

❏ **Secular humanism,** which makes humans the measuring rod of all existence, not God the Creator. Secular humanists glorify the human person and human achievement to the point that they exclude any religious faith or dependence on a supreme being.

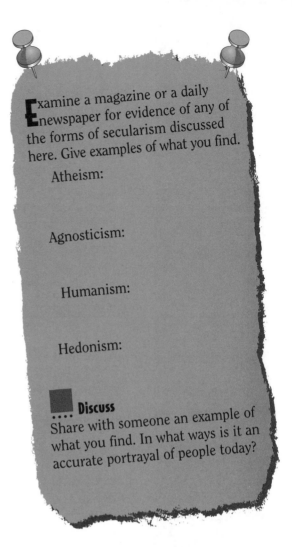

Examine a magazine or a daily newspaper for evidence of any of the forms of secularism discussed here. Give examples of what you find.

Atheism:

Agnosticism:

Humanism:

Hedonism:

Discuss
Share with someone an example of what you find. In what ways is it an accurate portrayal of people today?

❏ **Hedonism,** which makes pleasure the sole or chief good in life. The acquisition of sex, money, possessions, alcohol and other drugs, power and prestige, and the abject fear of getting old are various manifestations of hedonism.

The Desire for God

The human heart and the human mind direct us to God, who continually seeks us. God implanted in us a kind of honing device that directs us to discover and develop a personal relationship with him. In the words of Saint Augustine (A.D. 354–430),

"You have created us for yourself, O God, and our hearts are restless until they rest in you" *(Confessions)*.

We have an unquenchable thirst for happiness. We seek love and understanding. We seek possessions, pleasure, prestige, or whatever—none of these makes us *fully* happy. We always seem to need more. We can look to others for love and understanding, but somehow we search for more—for love and understanding other people cannot seem to give us. We believe that only God, who made us, can fill the insatiable hunger of our hearts for happiness, love, and understanding. Our inquisitive minds are also on a search, seeking truth. We want to know answers to questions, and especially the big questions: What is the *meaning* of life? Why am I here? Where am I going? Where does the world come from? What is worth living—and dying—for? What happens at death? These, and questions like them, are the really important questions. And God is the answer to all of them!

Coming to Know God

The hearts and minds of billions of human beings have "let go and let God" into their lives. Every culture known to us has believed in some supreme being to whom humans owe respect and allegiance. People in every culture and in every age have been and are convinced that God exists and that it is worth believing in him.

We believe that "by natural reason man can know God with certainty, on the basis of his works" (CCC, 50). Here are two of the "proofs" or arguments people have used to explain their decision to believe in God:

- ❏ **The existence of countless religions** shows that humans have a religious nature. The existence of the various sacrifices and rituals, prayers and meditations, beliefs and religious laws testify to the universal human quest for and belief in God.

- ❏ **The beauty, immensity, and symmetry of the world** point to a God who made all things and keeps them in existence. God is the master musician of the universe. You can hear his music in truth, beauty, and goodness.

The great medieval theologian Saint Thomas Aquinas (1225–1274) listed five proofs for the existence of God. In brief, his proofs claim that we can come to know with certainty that God exists by looking at the movement, becoming, contingency, and order and beauty in the world. For example, Saint Thomas points out that everything that exists is caused by something or someone else. Logically, if you reason back far enough, there has to be a source that was the very first cause of everything. This first cause must have always existed. Philosophy calls this first cause "God."

The world-famed statistician George Gallup (1901–1984) said God could be proved statistically by considering the human body. To claim that all the intricate functions of the human body are the result of chance is a statistical monstrosity!

What do you think?

- **The human search for and openness to truth and beauty show that we have a spiritual nature.** We recognize moral goodness. We possess freedom and a conscience. We deeply long for perfect happiness, love, and understanding. And remarkably, we can love, even to the point of giving our lives for another. The material universe cannot explain these realities. These spiritual activities—loving, thinking, choosing, understanding—can *only* have their origin in a spiritual being of infinite goodness.

- **Personal experience points to the presence of a "power" in our midst.** Reflect on your own experiences of awe and wonder in the face of a beautiful sunset or a newborn infant. Don't they speak to you of a power in the midst of the ordinary?

(CCC, 50–133)

Divine Revelation

Through the use of natural reason, we can come to know with certainty the existence of a divine being. However, left to ourselves, we cannot get a clear picture of what God is really like, who God really is. We need God to show, or reveal, himself to us. We need God to walk and talk with us.

Christians believe that God has walked and talked with us. We believe that God has revealed himself to us. The word *reveal* literally means "to unveil" or "to uncover." Christians believe that God has "unveiled" himself and "his plan of loving goodness" for us. We believe that God is gracious and loving and revealed himself by gradually communicating his own mystery in deeds and words.

God in Your Life

Put a ✓ next to any item that has been an experience of God's presence for you.

_____ While silently observing an awesome scene in nature, like a sunset over a lake

_____ In discovering a new idea or insight I never had before

_____ When someone expresses his or her love for me or when I express my love for someone

_____ In moments of prayer, Bible reading, or quiet reflection

_____ When someone forgives me

_____ When I stand for what is right, despite pressure to do otherwise

_____ When I hold a newborn baby

_____ In the quiet moments of meditation after receiving Holy Communion

_____

(Describe your own experience.)

Journal Writing: For you, what is the most convincing "proof" of God's existence?

We believe in divine **revelation.** "Through an utterly free decision, God has revealed himself and given himself to man" (CCC, 50). Christians believe that out of infinite love, God "unveiled" himself in human history and has spoken to us, lives among us, and invites us to live in **covenant** with him. The covenant is the wholehearted commitment between God and humans. It is God's promise to be faithful to us forever and our promise to be faithful to God.

Christians also believe that the fullest expression of God's love and communication to us is the gift of his Son, Jesus Christ. The writer of the Letter to the Hebrews sums up our faith this way:

In times past, God spoke in partial and various ways to our ancestors through the prophets; in these last days, he spoke to us through a son, whom he made heir of all things and through whom he created the universe, who is the refulgence of his glory, the very imprint of his being, and who sustains all things by his mighty word.

Hebrews 1:1–3

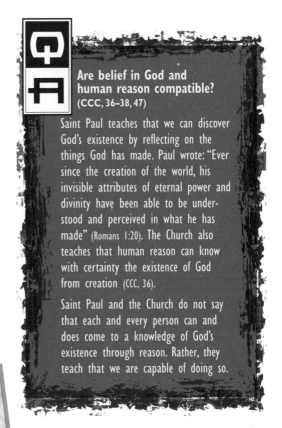

Are belief in God and human reason compatible? (CCC, 36–38, 47)

Saint Paul teaches that we can discover God's existence by reflecting on the things God has made. Paul wrote: "Ever since the creation of the world, his invisible attributes of eternal power and divinity have been able to be understood and perceived in what he has made" (Romans 1:20). The Church also teaches that human reason can know with certainty the existence of God from creation (CCC, 36).

Saint Paul and the Church do not say that each and every person can and does come to a knowledge of God's existence through reason. Rather, they teach that we are capable of doing so.

The Stages of Revelation

God, from the very beginning, invited us to live in covenant, or intimate communion, with him. We call the story of God's invitation and the human response to that invitation salvation history. Salvation history begins with God's generous creation of the world and our first parents, whom the creation story names Adam and Eve. After their sin, which we call original

sin, God remained faithful. He did not abandon humanity. God continued to invite humanity to live in friendship and communion with him. God promised to save us from our sin and redeem us, giving us hope of eternal life. God revealed this mystery, or plan of his goodness and faithful love and of salvation, through a series of covenants.

·············· Noah ··············

Sin shattered God's original plan and divided the unity of humanity into many separated and even hostile peoples. By means of a covenant with Noah, God reached out to a divided humanity that would remain in force as long as the world lasts. Its purpose was to eventually "gather into one the dispersed children of God" (John 11:52) through Jesus Christ the Lord.

Abraham

The revelation of God's plan to gather "the dispersed children of God" into one people continues through the covenant with the patriarch Abraham. "I will maintain my covenant with you and your descendants after you throughout the ages as an everlasting pact, to be your God and the God of your descendants after you" (Genesis 17:7). Abraham is the father of the Jewish people and "our father in faith." The descendants of Abraham were "called to prepare for that day when God would gather all his children into the unity of the Church" (CCC, 60; see Romans 11:17–18, 24).

Moses and the People of Israel

After the era of the patriarchs, God taught and guided the People of God through Moses. God revealed the laws of the Covenant to Moses and the Israelites so that "they would recognize him and serve him as the one living and true God, the provident Father and just judge, and so that they would look for the promised Savior" (CCC, 62; see *Dogmatic Constitution on Divine Revelation*, 3).

Prophets

Through Isaiah, Jeremiah, Ezekiel, and other prophets, God continued to unveil the mystery of his plan for us. The prophets spoke of the Messiah, who would come and establish a new and everlasting covenant in the hearts of all humans.

Jesus Christ

Jesus Christ is the "mediator and fullness" of God's revelation. He is the final Word of God, God's own Son. He lived among us, teaching us in words we could understand and actions we could observe. He is the fullness of God's revelation and his great love for us. In Christ God has established his covenant forever. To meet Jesus Christ is to meet the Father and the Spirit. By means of his passion, death, and resurrection-ascension, Jesus completed the Father's plan of salvation.

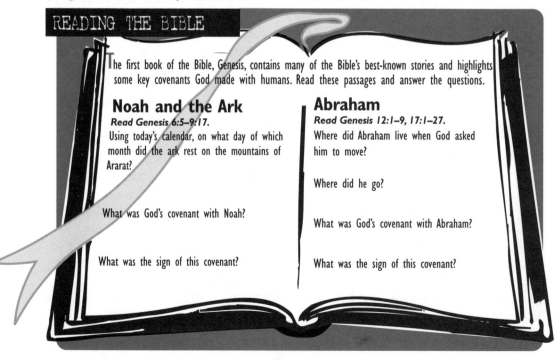

READING THE BIBLE

The first book of the Bible, Genesis, contains many of the Bible's best-known stories and highlights some key covenants God made with humans. Read these passages and answer the questions.

Noah and the Ark
Read Genesis 6:5–9:17.
Using today's calendar, on what day of which month did the ark rest on the mountains of Ararat?

What was God's covenant with Noah?

What was the sign of this covenant?

Abraham
Read Genesis 12:1–9, 17:1–27.
Where did Abraham live when God asked him to move?

Where did he go?

What was God's covenant with Abraham?

What was the sign of this covenant?

The Passing On of Divine Revelation

God speaks to us today of his saving plan through Sacred Scripture and the Sacred Tradition of the Church. Scripture and Tradition are a single sacred deposit of faith. They are two streams of the one fountain of divine revelation and are intimately united to each other.

Sacred
.... Scripture ....

The Bible, composed of the seventy-three books in both the Old and the New Testaments, is the inspired written Word of God. In **Sacred Scripture,** God speaks to us "in a human way."

Written under the inspiration of the Holy Spirit, the Sacred Scripture teaches the truth about God's revelation to us. This means that God is the author of Sacred Scripture. The Holy Spirit worked in and through the human authors.

The Old Testament passes God's revelation on to us through the Hebrews, or Israelites. The inspired writings of the Old Testament record a rich story of how God rescued the Israelites out of Egypt, led them to the Promised Land, and formed them into a nation and a religious community. They tell the story of how this people grew to know and worship the one true God, despite their many failings to abide by God's covenant. They especially testify to God's magnificent love and faithfulness to his promise to save all humanity through a messiah—whom we believe is our Lord and Savior, Jesus Christ, the Son of God become one of us.

Apostles' Creed

I believe in God,
    the Father almighty,
    creator of heaven and earth.
I believe in Jesus Christ,
    his only Son, our Lord.
He was conceived by the
    power of the Holy Spirit
    and born of the Virgin Mary.
He suffered under Pontius Pilate,
    was crucified, died, and was
    buried.
He descended into hell.
On the third day he rose again.
He ascended into heaven
    and is seated at the right
    hand of the Father.
He will come again to judge
    the living and the dead.
I believe in the Holy Spirit,
    the holy catholic Church,
    the communion of saints,
    the forgiveness of sins,
    the resurrection of the body,
    and the life everlasting.
                Amen.

The New Testament passes on to us the revelation of God made known through Jesus Christ. The writings of the New Testament center on the life and teachings of Jesus Christ and the faith of the early Christian community formed in his name. The New Testament Gospels are the very heart of the Bible. They provide the prime witness to the life and teachings of Jesus Christ.

Sacred
.... Tradition ....

Sacred Tradition is the living transmission of divine revelation through the community of God's people, the Church. Tradition hands on the Word of God, which the Lord and Spirit first gave to the apostles. The apostles "entrusted" this deposit of faith to the whole Church. The successors of the apostles (the bishops and pope), helped by the Holy Spirit, faithfully preserve, explain, and spread it throughout the world. This sacred teaching authority of the Church is called the **Magisterium.** The word *magisterium* comes from the Latin word *magister,* meaning "teacher."

We find this living Tradition in the Church's teaching, life, and worship. "What was handed on by the apostles comprises everything that serves to make the People of God live their lives in holiness and increase their faith. In this way the Church, in her doctrine, life and worship, perpetuates and transmits to every generation all that she herself is, all that she believes" (*Dogmatic Constitution on Divine Revelation,* 8).

Using a copy of the Nicene Creed, note one statement of our Catholic faith that it adds to the Apostles' Creed about each of the Persons of the Holy Trinity.

God the Father:

God the Son:

God the Holy Spirit:

(CCC, 142–175, 1814–1816)

Faith:
Responding to God

We come to recognize and respond to God's revelation because of the gift of **faith.** Scripture defines faith as "the realization of what is hoped for and evidence of things not seen" (Hebrews 11:1). Faith is a "gift from God." Faith calls us to a total life commitment to our loving God and to a resounding "yes" to the truths he has shared with us in Christ our Lord. This response is possible only by grace and the help of the Holy Spirit.

Qualities of Faith

❏ **Faith is a grace.** Like revelation, faith is God's free gift to us. The Holy Spirit imparts the gift of faith to us, empowering us to submit our intellects and wills to the self-revelation of God. Because of faith we can believe God's revealed truths because God himself has revealed them to us.

❏ **Faith is a free, human act.** No one is forced to embrace faith against his or her will. God invites us to freely respond to cooperate with his free gift of grace.

❏ **Faith is certain.** Faith is "founded on the word of God." But faith also invites us to grow in and understand God's word to us.

❏ **Faith is the beginning of eternal life.** Faith is necessary for salvation. When we cooperate with faith, we are on the path to eternal life—we choose to live our life in communion with God.

❏ **Faith is a virtue, a power, and a good habit.** Faith attracts and binds us to God—Father, Son, and Holy Spirit—in a relationship of love. It strengthens us to live with conviction, commitment, and trust in God's love for us.

The Creeds of the Church

We do not believe alone. Faith is more than the personal act of an individual believer.

We are called to believe as part of the community of the followers of Jesus Christ, the Church. As a gift from God, faith comes through the Church. "It is through the Church that we receive faith and new life in Christ by Baptism" (CCC, 168).

Believing, professing, and living our faith is an act of the Church, the community of God's people. While faith gives life to and supports and nourishes the individual Christian, we are called to live and profess our faith as a member of the People of God. "Each believer is thus a link in the great chain of believers" (CCC, 166).

The Church professes its belief in the **creed.** A creed is a statement of belief. The word *creed* derives from the Latin word *credere,* which means "to believe." Since its very beginning, the Church has summarized its faith in creeds, or summary statements of beliefs. The Apostles' Creed and the Nicene Creed are the two main creeds of the Church.

The Apostles' Creed dates to at least A.D. 390. Its name shows that the beliefs it summarizes are founded in the beliefs passed on to us by the apostles. A legend holds that each of the twelve articles of belief named in the Apostles' Creed is written by one of the apostles. What historians can show is that the Apostles' Creed is based on an early baptismal creed used in Rome in the second century A.D. Its substance is definitely rooted in apostolic faith.

The Nicene Creed comes from two important councils of the Church— the Council of Nicaea in A.D. 325 and the First Council of Constantinople in A.D. 381. This is the creed, or profession of faith, we profess together at Mass.

> **E**ach believer is thus a link in the great chain of believers.
>
> ॐ
>
> *Catechism of the Catholic Church,* 166

The substance of both the Apostles' Creed and the Nicene Creed includes three fundamental beliefs of great importance to Christians:

❏ The almighty and eternal God created all that exists.

❏ Jesus Christ is the Son of God-made-flesh. Born of the Virgin Mary, he died for our salvation and rose from the dead and ascended to heaven. He will come at the end of time to judge the living and the dead.

❏ The Risen Lord sent the Holy Spirit, the third Person of the Blessed Trinity, to give life to the Church. Through this one, holy, catholic, and apostolic Church, Christ dispenses the grace we need to reach eternal life.

When we pray "I believe . . . ," we are making a personal act of faith. When we pray "We believe . . . ," we are professing our faith as a community of faith. Whenever we profess our faith, we are professing it as a member of the Church, the People of God. We believe as a community of faith.

Professing our faith in a creed helps bind us to our sisters and brothers in the faith. Following the lead of the *Catechism of the Catholic Church,* this book will discuss the twelve major articles of the Apostles' Creed.

IMPORTANT TERMS TO KNOW

covenant—God's promise to be faithful to us forever and our promise to be faithful to God

creed—a formal summary statement of beliefs

faith—a theological virtue and gift of the Holy Spirit that enables us to respond to God and to believe the truths God has revealed because of his own authority

Magisterium—the teaching authority and responsibility of the Church to interpret authentically the faith contained in Sacred Scripture and Tradition

revelation—God's free gift of making himself known and giving himself to us by gradually communicating his own mystery in deeds and words

Sacred Scripture—the written inspired Word of God, consisting of the forty-six books of the Old Testament and the twenty-seven books of the New Testament

Sacred Tradition—the living transmission accomplished in the Holy Spirit by the Church. "The Church, in her doctrine, life and worship, perpetuates and transmits to every generation all that she herself is, all that she believes" (*Dogmatic Constitution on Divine Revelation,* 8).

secularism—a view of the world that focuses exclusively on the natural world and holds that the only means of knowing truth is through the natural sciences

CHAPTER SUMMARY

Saint Anselm of Canterbury (1033–1109) observed, "For I do not seek to understand that I may believe, but I believe in order to understand." In this chapter we learned that:

1. God is the source of true happiness. Some people, like secularists, atheists, humanists, and hedonists, do not put their faith in God but seek happiness in other "gods."

2. Through the use of reason, we can know with certainty that God exists. It is reasonable to believe and trust in God.

3. We believe that God has revealed himself to us. God has revealed himself to us in stages. Jesus Christ, our Lord and Savior, the Son of God-made-flesh, is God's fullest and most complete revelation.

4. Faith is God's free gift to us. It invites us and enables us to respond freely to God's revelation.

5. The creeds of the Church express our faith. The Apostles' Creed and the Nicene Creed are the two main creeds of the Church.

6. Divine revelation is handed on to us through Sacred Scripture and Sacred Tradition. Sacred Scripture is the inspired Word of God written down by the People of God. It contains the Old Testament and the New Testament. Sacred Tradition is the living transmission of the Word of God through the doctrine, life, and worship of the Church.

EXPLORING OUR CATHOLIC FAITH

1. Listening to God's Word

The Psalms are the prayer book of the Old Testament. Throughout the ages, they have remained a fruitful resource for prayer that ranges the gamut of human emotions. Read Psalms 8, 29, 65, and 104. List at least five ways God speaks to the psalmist.

2. Understanding the Teachings of the Catholic Church

In the *Dogmatic Constitution on Divine Revelation*, we read: "The divinely revealed realities, which are contained and presented in the text of sacred Scripture, have been written down under the inspiration of the Holy Spirit" (11). With a few of your classmates research the meaning of the phrase "under the inspiration of the Holy Spirit." Share your findings with the whole group.

3. Reflecting on Our Catholic Faith

Read and reflect on the words of Saint Anselm of Canterbury. What do they say to you about your own search to become a person of faith? Write your thoughts in your journal.

4. Living Our Catholic Faith

"Each believer is thus a link in the great chain of believers" (CCC, 166). What can you say or do to be a "link" in the great chain of believers? Brainstorm your ideas with your group. Choose one of your ideas and live it out.

CHAPTER 2

God, Our Loving Father and Creator

"Hear, O Israel! The LORD is our God, the LORD alone!
Therefore, you shall love the LORD, your God,
with all your heart, and with all your soul,
and with all your strength."

DEUTERONOMY 6:4–5

What Do You Think?

In the space provided, write "A" if you agree with the statement, "D" if you disagree with it, or "N" if you have no opinion about it. Discuss your responses.

_____ 1. The literal meaning of Yahweh is "Lord."

_____ 2. The Old Testament contains forty-six books.

_____ 3. All God's creatures have equal dignities.

_____ 4. Devils do not really exist; they are simply symbolic of the presence of evil in the world.

_____ 5. Men and women were created for companionship.

Two little children, Sarah and Tommy, were receiving their first lessons from the Bible—the Genesis account of creation and the Adam and Eve story. After reading the appropriate Scripture passages, the elderly teacher asked Sarah what she thought of the stories. Sarah responded, "I love them. They're so exciting. You never know what God's going to do next!"

The teacher then instructed her students to draw a picture of Adam and Eve in the Garden of Eden. Tommy busily created his masterpiece—an elderly, bearded gentleman driving a rusty old car. In the backseat sat two scantily clad passengers. The teacher was a bit confused. During show-and-tell, she asked the budding artist what the picture was supposed to represent.

"Well," Tommy somewhat indignantly exclaimed, "doesn't the Bible tell us that God drove Adam and Eve out of the Garden of Eden?"

The Sacred Scriptures are God's Word. What questions do you have about reading the Bible?

KEY TERMS

canon of the Bible

divine providence

dogma

original sin

Trinity

Yahweh

The two budding theologians in our story had some interesting insights about God. Little Sarah was surely correct in saying that the biblical God was a God full of surprises, no doubt because God is an unfathomable Mystery. This chapter will highlight a brief exploration of the Old Testament and the biblical teachings about God the Father Almighty and God's creation.

(*Catechism of the Catholic Church,* 109–130, 203–209)

God's Inspired Word

The Bible tells the marvelous story of how God, who is Love and Truth, gradually revealed himself, first to the people of the Old Covenant and, finally and most fully, in Jesus Christ, the New Covenant.

The Name of God

One way God made himself known was to reveal his name. A name expresses a person's identity, their very essence. By revealing his name to be **Yahweh,** which means "I am," or "I am he who is," or "I am who am," or "I am who I am," God revealed that he is the one who creates all that is and keeps it all in existence. God is always present with his people, "a merciful and gracious God, slow to anger and rich in kindness and fidelity" (Exodus 34:6).

At the same time, the name *I am* reveals that God is profound. Moses sensed this when he took off his shoes and bowed in God's presence. The great prophet knew that he was in the presence of a holy, omnipotent, almighty, and awesome Being. So holy is God—and God's name—that the

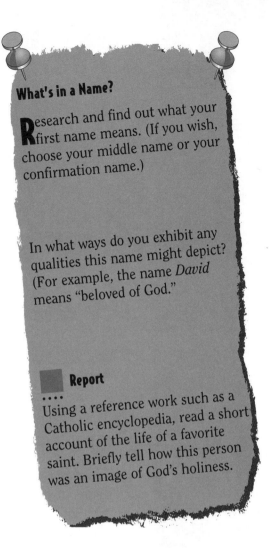

What's in a Name?

Research and find out what your first name means. (If you wish, choose your middle name or your confirmation name.)

In what ways do you exhibit any qualities this name might depict? (For example, the name *David* means "beloved of God."

Report

• • • •

Using a reference work such as a Catholic encyclopedia, read a short account of the life of a favorite saint. Briefly tell how this person was an image of God's holiness.

Jewish people, even today, do not speak the name Yahweh. In its place they use the divine title *Lord* (in Hebrew "Adonai") whenever YAHWEH appears. Christians use this title to acknowledge that Jesus is God—"Jesus is Lord!"

Sacred Scripture

This story of the revelation of the mystery of God and God's loving plan for creation and humankind is told throughout the Scriptures. Its climax is the revelation of God's saving love for us—Jesus Christ, our Lord and Savior, whose passion, death, resurrection, and glorification conquered sin and overcame death.

In chapter 1 we discussed that the Bible is the inspired Word of God. This means that, in a very real sense, God is the author of Scripture. The Church teaches:

> To compose the sacred books, God chose certain men who, all the while he employed them in this task, made full use of their powers and faculties so that, though he acted in them and by them, it was as true authors that they consigned to writing whatever he wanted written, and no more. *Dogmatic Constitution on Divine Revelation,* 11

The word *Bible* means "the book." It is a collection of various types of writings (the word *scriptures* means "writings") that pass on to us what God has revealed about the mystery of God and God's loving plan for us. When we examine the writings in the Bible, we discover many literary genres such as history, religious stories, poetry, prayer, proverbs, letters, gospels, and parables. In reading the inspired Scripture, we must be attentive above all to what God wants to reveal through the sacred author. What comes from the Spirit cannot be fully understood except by the Spirit's action. Each type of writing passes on to us, in its own unique way, the truth of God's Word.

When we read or hear the Word of God proclaimed to us, it is important to know the type of writing we are reading or listening to. This helps us to under-stand what the sacred writer, under the inspiration of God, was trying to pass on to us.

The Old Testament

The writings that are officially recognized by the Church are called the **canon of Sacred Scripture.** Catholics recognize forty-six books in the Old Testament and twenty-seven books in the New Testament. For both Jews and Christians, Sacred Scripture is the holy Word of God. Christians believe that both the Old Testament and the New Testament are the inspired, holy Word of God. Both are venerated as the "true Word of God" and an indispensable part of Scripture.

We divide the Old Testament writings into four major categories: the Pentateuch, historical writings, wisdom writings, and the writings of the prophets.

········· The Pentateuch ·········

The five books of the Pentateuch (*pentateuch* meaning "five") deal with God's covenant of love with the Jewish people. This collection of writings is also called the Torah, or Law, because it sets down Israel's responsibilities for living the covenant. The Pentateuch includes these five books: Genesis, Exodus, Leviticus, Numbers, and Deuteronomy.

······· Historical Writings ·······

The collection of historical books tells of God's saving activity in the history of the People of Israel. The sixteen historical books include Joshua, Judges, Ruth, 1 Samuel, 2 Samuel, 1 Kings, 2 Kings, 1 Chronicles, 2 Chronicles, Ezra, Nehemiah, Tobit, Judith, Esther, 1 Maccabees, and 2 Maccabees.

········ Wisdom Writings ········

The wisdom literature contains a variety of prayers, poems, and wise sayings that reflect on ways to live a faithful, good life. The wisdom literature includes these seven books: Job, Psalms, Proverbs, Ecclesiastes, Song of Songs, Wisdom, and Ecclesiasticus (Sirach).

····The Writings of the Prophets····

The writings of the prophets have the constant theme of calling the Israelites to repent and be faithful to living God's covenant with them. The sixteen prophetic books include Isaiah, Jeremiah, Lamentations, Baruch, Ezekiel, Daniel, Hosea, Joel, Amos, Obadiah, Jonah, Micah, Nahum, Habakkuk, Zephaniah, Haggai, Zechariah, and Malachi.

··········The Covenant··········

The heart of the Old Testament Scriptures is the covenant binding and bonding God and the people of Israel. Out of sheer love, God made solemn promises to the people of Israel to be "their God," always faithful and true to them. For their part, the Jews were to worship God as the only true God, the source of all that exists. They were to live the heart of the covenant, summarized in the Ten Commandments. Living the Law would form them into the people of God and make them a special witness among the nations to the one true God.

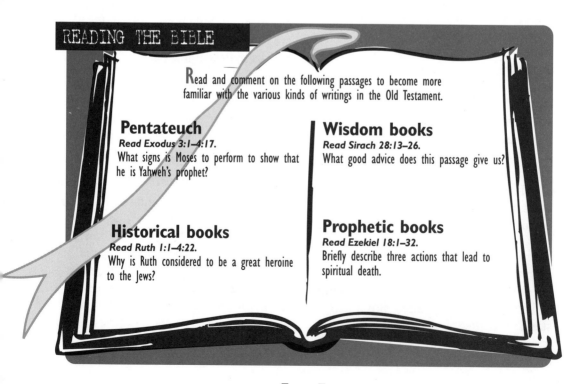

READING THE BIBLE

Read and comment on the following passages to become more familiar with the various kinds of writings in the Old Testament.

Pentateuch
Read Exodus 3:1–4:17.
What signs is Moses to perform to show that he is Yahweh's prophet?

Wisdom books
Read Sirach 28:13–26.
What good advice does this passage give us?

Historical books
Read Ruth 1:1–4:22.
Why is Ruth considered to be a great heroine to the Jews?

Prophetic books
Read Ezekiel 18:1–32.
Briefly describe three actions that lead to spiritual death.

The Old Testament, however, tells about the infidelity of God's people to God. Often they fall back into the worship of the false gods of their neighbors—the gods of the rain and the gods and goddesses of fertility. God, Yahweh, however, never abandons his people. He sends prophets to instruct, admonish, and guide them. And he remains faithful to the covenant when the Israelites are carried off as captives into Babylonia. He frees them and eventually restores them to Israel.

We Christians believe that the climax and fulfillment of God's covenant is Jesus Christ, the Messiah and Savior, promised by God. The Son of God takes on flesh and becomes one of us. In the Paschal mystery of his death-resurrection-ascension, the final, everlasting covenant with humanity is established.

(CCC, 198–379)

We Believe in God, the Father

What do we mean when we profess, "I believe in God"? The Bible tells us that God has revealed himself to be one who is merciful and gracious, who is Truth and Love, who is Father, Son, and Holy Spirit, a Holy Trinity—one God in three Persons.

- ❏ **God is Truth.** God's Word is faithful, trustworthy, and true. He is the source of all knowledge. Jesus came to bear testimony to the Truth so we can come to know the one living God who loves us.

- ❏ **God is Love.** God's love is like that of a father for a son but immeasurably greater. Likewise, God's love far surpasses a mother's love for her

children or a groom's love for his new bride. "God is love" (1 John 4:8). The very nature of God is to love as a Trinity of Persons, inviting us to share in that love.

- ❏ **God is Holy Trinity: Father, Son, and Holy Spirit.** The central belief of Christians is that the one God is three Persons. No truth about God is more central to our faith than God is **Trinity,** that there is one God who is three equal Persons: Father, Son, and Holy Spirit. This mystery of our faith, revealed by God, tells us that God is an infinite community of love, a unity-in-community and a community-in-unity.

Human reason cannot discover this profound mystery of God. God alone can tell us this about himself and he has revealed it to us. Jesus teaches us that God is Father (John 17:1).

Symbols of Faith

Two interwoven equilateral triangles (a Trinitarian symbol) form the *Creator's Star.* The six points represent the six days of creation. This symbol is also called *David's Star* after the shape of David's shield.

Think of a symbol that you might use to help others gain some insight into the mystery of the Holy Trinity. Create your symbol here.

Jesus tells us that the Holy Spirit will teach, guide, and defend us in the truth (John 14:17, 26; 16:13).

❏ **God is Father Almighty.** The Apostles' Creed only names one of God's attributes, his omnipotence. God's almighty power, however, is not arbitrary. God's power is mysterious. God is loving, merciful, and gracious. He created us freely and out of love. He renews his covenant freely and out of love. The Father sends his only Son freely and out of love. He saves us and offers us the gift of everlasting life and love freely and out of love.

Creator of Heaven and Earth

The first verse of the Bible tells us that in the beginning it was God who created the heavens and the earth (Genesis 1:1). This remarkable passage affirms that God alone is the Creator of all that exists, and it is God who keeps it in existence.

Based on the biblical record and the teaching of Tradition, the Church proclaims these truths about God's magnificent creation:

❏ God created the world out of wisdom and love to show forth and communicate his glory and that creatures share in his very life and love—in his truth, goodness, and beauty. Creation of the world and humans is the first proclamation of God's "loving plan of goodness," which finds its goal in the new creation in Christ.

❏ God is infinitely greater than his creation. God alone freely, directly, and without any help created an orderly and good world out of nothing. No preexisting matter was present before God created the world. God's awesome creative power is good, so all that God makes is good.

❏ God is a mystery totally beyond us. At the same time, God is always present with us, upholding and keeping creation in existence by his Word, the Son, and by his Creator Spirit, the giver of life. While we say the work of creation is the work of the Father, it is a truth of our faith that the work of creation is the work of the Trinity because the divine persons are inseparable.

❏ God guides creation through divine providence. **Divine providence** is God's ordering creation through his "loving plan of goodness."

What the Documents Say

Read and reflect on this teaching of the Church.

The eternal Father, in accordance with the utterly gratuitous and mysterious design of his wisdom and goodness, created the whole universe, and chose to raise up men to share in his own divine life.

Dogmatic Constitution on the Church, 2

How does it help you set goals for your life?

God lovingly and mercifully watches over everything he has made, guiding creatures on their journey to their final goal—eternal life with God.

❑ God created humans in his own image and likeness. Every person has this profound dignity. God made us all—regardless of sex, race, nationality, or ethnic origin—to be his children, sisters and brothers in one family. We are endowed with both a body and a soul. Our spiritual and immortal soul is created immediately by God. It empowers us with a spiritual nature that enables us to think, to discern right from wrong, and to love as God loves us. Though we had a beginning, we are immortal in the sense that we will never cease to exist.

❑ God created humans to be male and female out of love and for love. This reveals that God made us for companionship, to depend on and love each other. God made us with the same dignity—male and female—both equally good.

❑ Humans are the summit of God's creation. We are in solidarity with each other and with all of God's creatures. We are called to depend on one another and to respect the beauty of God's universe. We have the responsibility to develop—not destroy—God's creation for the good and well-being of everyone.

Maker of All That Is Seen and Unseen

Both the Bible and Tradition attest to the existence of angels. For example, the angel Gabriel announced Jesus' birth to Mary, and angels witnessed Jesus' birth. They comforted him during his trials in the desert and ministered to him in the Garden of Gethsemane. The New Testament also tells us that angels were present at Jesus' resurrection and ascension into heaven, spiritual beings created by God who glorify God without ceasing and who serve his saving plans for other creatures.

Catholics and other Christians have traditionally held that each of us has a guardian angel to watch over us, especially in times of temptation. Catholics celebrate the feast of Guardian Angels on October 2. September 29 is the feast day of Saints Michael, Raphael, and Gabriel, the only angels named in Sacred Scripture.

We believe that angels are personal, immortal, and can think and love. Like humans, they had an opportunity to love and accept God or reject him. Some angels lovingly worshiped God. Other angels freely turned to evil by radically and irrevocably rejecting God and his reign. Scripture and Tradition teach that Satan, which means "deceiver," and the fallen angels exist. They are also known as devils, from a word meaning "slanderer."

Genesis tells us of a serpent tempting Adam and Eve; and Revelation reports a symbolic battle in the heavens between good and evil angels. In his ministry, Jesus often encountered evil spirits. He also taught that his Father's kingdom would triumph over demons.

Satan and evil are great mysteries our minds can never fully fathom. However, the good news of the Gospel is that Jesus, our Lord and Savior, has triumphed over Satan, evil, and their worst effect—death! This good news of the Gospel of Jesus Christ gives us the hope to help us cope with the mystery of evil and suffering.

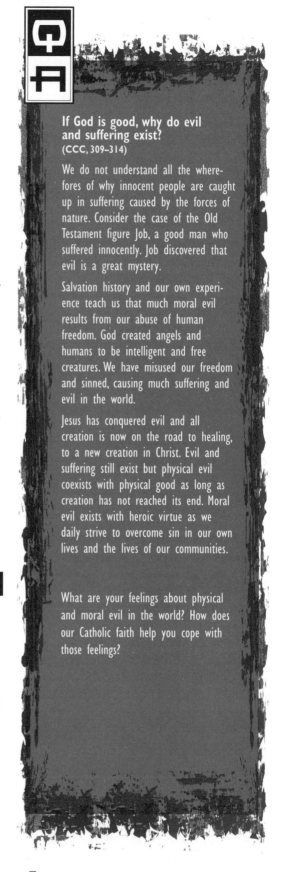

If God is good, why do evil and suffering exist?
(CCC, 309–314)

We do not understand all the wherefores of why innocent people are caught up in suffering caused by the forces of nature. Consider the case of the Old Testament figure Job, a good man who suffered innocently. Job discovered that evil is a great mystery.

Salvation history and our own experience teach us that much moral evil results from our abuse of human freedom. God created angels and humans to be intelligent and free creatures. We have misused our freedom and sinned, causing much suffering and evil in the world.

Jesus has conquered evil and all creation is now on the road to healing, to a new creation in Christ. Evil and suffering still exist but physical evil coexists with physical good as long as creation has not reached its end. Moral evil exists with heroic virtue as we daily strive to overcome sin in our own lives and the lives of our communities.

What are your feelings about physical and moral evil in the world? How does our Catholic faith help you cope with those feelings?

(CCC, 385-412)

The Fall and Original Sin

In the Genesis account of Adam and Eve, we note that humans are created in God's image and likeness. They were created in a state of original holiness. They were God's friends and were on intimate terms with him. They were in "paradise."

However, just as God created angels as free beings, he gave our first parents

the free choice to accept or reject his love. The scriptural account of the Fall uses figurative language to tell the sad story of our first parents' abuse of this freedom of choice by disobeying God and failing to rely on his goodness.

This original sin had consequences. It caused the immediate loss of the grace of original holiness, which we call **original sin.** It set humankind against God and began a search for happiness apart from God. This broken relationship caused disharmony between nature and human beings. Human nature was now weakened in its powers; it became subject to ignorance, suffering, the inclination to sin, and death. It also caused our alienation from one another.

After the Fall, sin became universal in human history. Original sin affects all humans. We have inherited a fallen human nature, deprived of original justice and holiness. Original sin is now transmitted to future generations.

Though we inherit it, original sin is not an actual sin we personally commit. What it means is that we are born into a condition where we are inclined to surrender to the powers of evil in the world.

Salvation history constantly tells the story of God's fidelity to his unfaithful creatures. The prophet Hosea compared God to a faithful husband who refused to abandon Israel, an unfaithful wife. Similarly, the Song of Songs fervently compares God's love for his people to that of an intense, passionate lover who knows no limits in loving his wife, Israel.

God's love reveals itself in deeds. He rescued the Jews from Pharaoh, sustained them for forty years, gave them a land and a king, and returned them to the Promised Land after their captivity. Moreover, God promised to send a Messiah, a true savior who would comfort us and fix our relationship with God.

God kept his promise by sending his only Son, Jesus Christ. He overcame the effects of original sin by dying and rising for us. Our own efforts cannot liberate us from this condition. The Gospel ("good news") of Christ Jesus is that his coming has won far greater blessings than those which original sin has taken from us. God's Son, Jesus Christ, and the Spirit of God, the Sanctifier, have the power to free us from the clutches of sin.

REVIEW

IMPORTANT TERMS TO KNOW

canon of Sacred Scripture—the Church's official list of biblical books considered inspired by God; the Catholic Bible contains forty-six Old Testament books and twenty-seven New Testament books

divine providence—God's loving and watchful guidance over his creatures on their way to their final goal and perfection

original sin—the first sin by which Adam lost his state of original holiness and justice he received from God, not only for himself but for all human beings; the state or condition of sin into which all people are born since the time of Adam's turning away from God

Trinity—the central belief and dogma of the Christian faith; one God in three divine persons—Father, Son, and Holy Spirit—inseparable and equal in what they are and also inseparable in what they do

Yahweh—the sacred Hebrew name for God, which means "I am who am"; it especially refers to God as the loving Creator of the universe and the origin of all being and life

CHAPTER SUMMARY

Father Charles Foucauld wrote: Father, "Let only your will be done in me and in all Your creatures—I wish no more than this, Lord." In this chapter we learned that:

1. God is the source of all being. He created to reveal and share his love. He is one, unique, merciful, gracious, living, and faithful. God is totally beyond humans; at the same time, God is present to us.

2. The forty-six Old Testament books recount the story of God's covenant with his people.

3. Belief in the mystery of the Holy Trinity—one God in three divine Persons—is the central belief of the Church.

4. God created us in his image and likeness. We have been created with a body and soul. We have the ability to think and to love. We are called to know, love, and serve God.

5. The first humans, Adam and Eve, rejected God through an act of disobedience. We call this original sin.

6. Evil and suffering in our world resulted from original sin.

7. God did not abandon humans after the sin of our first parents. He promised to send a Messiah, his Son, our Lord and Savior, Jesus Christ. His grace far surpasses evil, sin, and death.

EXPLORING OUR CATHOLIC FAITH

1. Listening to God's Word

The Church readily acknowledges that the biblical creation stories are not scientific treatises. What the biblical authors were interested in passing on to us was the religious truth. Read Genesis 1:1–2:4a (First Creation Story), Genesis 2:4b–25 (Second Creation Story), and Genesis 3:1–24 (The Story of the Fall). What religious truths do these readings teach about God? About humankind? About good and evil? How do the details of the stories do this?

2. Understanding the Teachings of the Catholic Church

The bishops at the Second Vatican Council in the *Pastoral Constitution on the Church in the Modern World* taught: "From the beginning 'male and female he created them' (see Genesis 1:27). This partnership of man and woman constitutes the first form of communion between persons . . . and if he does not enter into relations with others he can neither live nor develop his gifts" (12). Discuss with another person what this statement teaches. In what ways does it reflect the decisions we make. From what you see, hear, or read, do you think this truth is truly understood?

3. Reflecting on Our Catholic Faith

Reflect on this insight: "God can take the place of anything, but nothing can take the place of God." In what ways does it apply to your life? Write your reflections in your journal.

4. Living Our Catholic Faith

God calls us to turn to him alone as our first origin and our ultimate goal, and neither to prefer anything to him nor to substitute anything for him (CCC, 229). Form into groups and brainstorm ten ways today's teens can help one another live this truth of our faith. Discuss these lists with the entire group.

CHAPTER 3

Jesus Christ, the Son of God

For God so loved the world
that he gave his only Son.

JOHN 3:16

What Do You Think?

In the space below, write what you have learned the Church teaches about Jesus. Then write any questions you might have about Jesus.

Lawrence Le Shan recounts a story of an old monk who prayed fervently for many years for a vision from God to help his faith. The monk almost gave up hope, but one day he did receive a vision that was giving him much spiritual joy. Unfortunately, in the middle of his vision the bell of the monastery rang, calling him to feed the poor.

Torn between his vision and his duty, the monk reluctantly went to feed the poor. After an hour of ministering to them, he returned to his room. To his astonishment, the Lord was there as bright as day. With tears in his eyes, the monk dropped to his knees in thanksgiving. Then Jesus said to him, "My dear brother, had you not left to feed the hungry, I would have departed from you! But because you served me in the least of your sisters and brothers, I have remained here with you."

What does this story say to you about Jesus and his work among us?

The wise monk knew that the Lord remains with us today through each person, but in a special way through the poor, the suffering, the outcast in our midst (Matthew 25:34–41). With the eyes of faith, we proclaim Jesus as our Lord and Savior. In this chapter, we will examine the principal Catholic beliefs about Jesus Christ, whom we profess to be true God and true man.

(Catechism of the Catholic Church, 124–127, 422–451, 461–465)

The Good News: God Has Sent His Son

By the grace of the Holy Spirit, we confess our faith in Jesus **Christ,** the Son of God, who "took on flesh" and lived among us. Through the Paschal mystery of his suffering, death, resurrection, and ascension, he freed us from sin and the power of evil. We believe we will live with him forever by power of the Spirit.

The Witness of Historians

Evidence for the existence of Jesus is not limited to the witness of the early believers in Jesus. The Roman historians Pliny the Younger (A.D. 23–79), Tacitus (ca. A.D. 55–117), and Suetonius (ca. A.D. 119) refer to Jesus and his followers as the Christians. Josephus (ca. A.D. 37–100), an important first-century Jewish historian, also mentions Jesus in two of his writings.

The Witness of the Gospels

The twenty-seven books of the New Testament, written under the inspiration of the Holy Spirit, proclaim the Church's faith in Jesus Christ, the Son of God become man, who freed us from

Jesus and Human History

Blaise Pascal (1623–1662), a French scientist and philosopher, wrote, "Jesus is the center of all, and the goal to which all tends." What do the abbreviations A.D., B.C., C.E., and B.C.E. mean? What significance do they have for human history? What do they tell us about the place of Jesus Christ in history?

sin, reconciled us with God and one another, and gave us the promise of eternal life with God.

The four canonical **Gospels,** however, are the best witnesses to Jesus. Each beyond question attests to Jesus' existence. Each of the Gospels is a unique statement of the faith of the early Church regarding who Jesus is and what he did.

The Gospels contain certain words and teachings that bear the stamp of an outstanding, unique teacher, Jesus of Nazareth. He lived among us, was executed, rose from the dead, ascended to his Father, and sent the Holy Spirit to be our Helper and Teacher.

The four Gospels are the heart of the New Testament—indeed the heart of the entire Scriptures—because they pass on to us the key elements of the Church's faith in our Lord. At the heart of the Gospels, in turn, is the proclamation of the good news that God sent his Son, who:

❑ was conceived by the power of the Holy Spirit and born of the **Virgin Mary;**

- ❏ suffered, died, and was buried;
- ❏ rose from the dead;
- ❏ ascended into heaven;
- ❏ sent the Holy Spirit; and
- ❏ will return again in glory at the end of time.

The Formation of the Gospels

The Church teaches that the written Gospels resulted at the end of a three-stage process: the life and teaching of Jesus, the passing on of the Church's faith in Jesus by word of mouth (oral tradition), and the writing down of the Church's faith in Jesus Christ.

Stage 1:
... The Life and Teaching of Jesus ...

The period of Jesus' life and teaching lasted from the birth of Jesus around 4 to 6 B.C., to his death around A.D. 30 or 33. At the center of Jesus' life on earth is the **Paschal mystery**—the passion-death-resurrection-ascension of Jesus. The Gospels faithfully hand on what Jesus taught and did for our salvation.

Stage 2:
.... Oral Tradition ....

The period of oral tradition lasted from Jesus' ascension until the time the Gospels were written.

Enlightened by the Holy Spirit, the apostles and early disciples faithfully and without error passed on the revelation who Jesus is and what he taught and did. They passed on this faith through prayers, stories, testimonies, homilies, hymns, proclamations, and catechetical lessons. Some of these traditions took written shape during this time, but they were not compiled into the written Gospels until later.

Stage 3:
.... Written Gospels ....

Many scholars think the Gospels were written over a period of about thirty-five years. Common opinion holds that the Gospel of Mark was written between 65 and 70, Matthew and Luke between 75 and 85, and John between 90 and 100.

READING THE BIBLE

The Infancy Narratives

We can see these different perspectives at work in how Matthew and Luke present the birth of Jesus. The mysteries of Jesus' life in these chapters of Matthew and Luke reveal much about his mission.
(CCC, 525–534; 563–564)

Read Matthew 1:18–25 and Luke 1:26–38.
After reading these two infancy narratives, list five differences and five similarities between them.

Drawing on the oral traditions and some materials already written down, the **evangelists** (the word *evangelist* means "writer of the good news") adapted materials for a particular audience for whom the Gospel was written. For example, Mark's Gospel was probably written in Rome during a time of persecution when the Christians were being tempted to give up their faith in Jesus.

Each evangelist had a particular audience and purpose in mind when he wrote his version of the good news. For example, Mark stressed Jesus as the Suffering Servant. Matthew underscored Jesus as the New Lawgiver. Luke highlighted Jesus as the Universal Messiah. John presented Jesus as God's Unique Word who came to be the Way, Truth, and Life.

Each evangelist hoped to strengthen the faith of the Christians by telling them the meaning of Jesus' death and resurrection.

The New Testament Letters and Other Writings

In addition to the four Gospels, the New Testament contains twenty-three other writings named by the Church to be written under the inspiration of the Holy Spirit. These writings are:

.... Acts of the Apostles ....

Written by the author of Luke's Gospel, the Acts of the Apostles recounts the life and growth of the Church from the first Christian Pentecost until the arrest of Paul in Rome around A.D. 63.

...The Epistles and Letters of Paul...

The New Testament contains thirteen letters or epistles that are attributed by name to the apostle Paul. Paul wrote

Jesus Symbols

Christians also passed on their faith in Jesus Christ through the use of symbols. One of these symbols is that of a fish.

This was a secret sign used by early persecuted Christians to designate themselves as followers of Jesus. The Greek word for fish is ΙΧΘΥΣ, which is an anagram for "Jesus Christ, God's Son, Savior."

Ιησους = Jesus
Χριστος = Christ
Θεου = of God
Υυιος = Son
Σωτερ = Savior

Create your own symbol to express your faith in Jesus.

about particular theological and practical issues that faced the early Church. All his writings highlight the importance of faith in Jesus Christ. These include Romans, 1 and 2 Corinthians, Galatians, Philippians, 1 Thessalonians, and Philemon.

Six other letters bear the name Paul but probably were written by his disciples. These are Ephesians, Colossians, 2 Thessalonians, 1 and 2 Timothy, and Titus.

Hebrews and the
..... Seven Catholic Epistles .....

Hebrews is more like a sermon. Its major focus is the priesthood of Jesus Christ. Written primarily for Jewish Christians, Hebrews passes on the Church's faith in God's revelation that the worship of the Old Covenant has been fulfilled by the sacrifice of Jesus Christ.

The seven Catholic epistles are the letters of James; 1 and 2 Peter; 1, 2, and 3 John; and Jude. These writings encourage the universal ("catholic") Church to remain faithful to Jesus Christ and to faithfully live as his Christian followers.

..... The Book of Revelation .....

This highly symbolic work—also known by its Greek name, the Apocalypse—encourages Christians under persecution to remain faithful to Jesus Christ.

Titles of Jesus

Jesus' name and his titles reveal much about his identity and our Christian belief about him.

The name *Jesus:* The Hebrew name *Jesus* means "God saves." Jesus' very name reveals his mission of salvation for all people. An ancient Easter Christian prayer, the Jesus Prayer, expresses our faith in Jesus: "Lord Jesus Christ, Son of God, have mercy on me, a sinner."

The title *Christ:* *Christ* is the Greek word for the Hebrew title *Messiah,* meaning "anointed one." God's Spirit anointed Jesus to bring about our salvation through a threefold office of prophet, priest, and king. As God's Prophet, Jesus reveals his Father and proclaims salvation. As the High Priest, Jesus gave his life on the altar of the cross so we may live. As true King,

I n Mark 8:27–30 Jesus asks his disciples what people are saying about him. The views in his day were many—that Jesus was John the Baptist, Elijah, or another prophet. Read and reflect on these faith statements.

❑ Jesus is my Lord and Savior.

❑ Jesus is the Way, the Truth, and the Life.

❑ Jesus is the Messiah.

❑ Jesus is the Son of God.

❑ Jesus is our Savior, who died and rose from the dead to give us eternal life.

What do you think?

Complete these statements and discuss your responses with friends and family.

My favorite title for Jesus is (compose a new title if you wish)

This is my favorite because

Jesus compassionately rules the universe and, through the Spirit, guides us to be one with the Father and one another as he is.

The title *Son of God:* This title expresses our faith in the unique and eternal relationship between Jesus and his Father. Jesus proclaims himself the Son of God (John 10:36) who is one with the Father (John 10:30). He is the only Son of the Father. He is God himself. Many times the Gospels proclaim Jesus to be God's unique Son. At Jesus' baptism (Mark 1:11) and transfiguration (Matthew 17:5), the Father calls Jesus his "beloved Son." Peter acknowledges him to be "the Messiah, the Son of the living God" (Matthew 16:16).

The title *Suffering Servant:* Jesus was a Suffering Servant who takes on the sins of his people and redeems them. He taught: "[T]he Son of Man did not come to be served but to serve and to give his life as a ransom for many" (Matthew 20:28).

The title *Lord:* The title *Lord* translates the Greek *kyrios,* which in turn designated the divinity of Israel's God. When early Christians called Jesus *Lord,* they were proclaiming their belief that Jesus is truly God. They were saying that the honor and glory that are due God are equally due Jesus.

The title *Word of God:* The opening verse of John's Gospel proclaims Jesus to be God's Word: "In the beginning was the Word, / and the Word was with God, / and the Word was God" (John 1:1). Equal to God, always existing with God, "the Word became flesh / and made his dwelling among us, / and we saw his glory, / the glory as of the Father's only Son, / full of grace and truth" (John 1:14).

The title *Son of Man:* Jesus typically chose this title when speaking of himself. Found in the Old Testament Book of Daniel (7:13), this title refers to Jesus as a human—one who is like us and will suffer for and serve all people.

(CCC, 456–478, 484–487, 495)

What We Believe about Jesus

The Church, with the guidance and help of the Holy Spirit, has since its very beginning deepened its understanding of Jesus and his work among us. Here is a summary of what the Church believes about Jesus Christ.

The Incarnation of the Son of God

Our belief in the Incarnation is a **dogma** of the Church.

The word *incarnation* means "take on flesh." The dogma of the **Incarnation** expresses our faith that the eternal Son of God, the second Person of the Holy Trinity, took on flesh and became fully man without giving up his divinity. We believe that Jesus Christ is true God and true man; he is fully human and fully divine.

The Incarnation is a great mystery of God's love. We believe that Jesus assumed our nature, wanting to make us sharers in his divinity. This is a mystery of our faith that we can never fully understand.

Jesus Christ Is the Only Son of God

Jesus is "eternally begotten of the Father, God from God, Light from Light, true God from true God, begotten, not made, one in Being with the Father" (Nicene Creed).

All Things Were Made Through the Son

The Son always existed with the Father and shares his nature. Thus, he also shares in the creation of the world (John 1:1–4). To underscore this point, the Council of Nicaea distinguished between "begotten" and "created." The Father "begets" the Son and "creates" the world. In other words, the Son always existed. The Son was always in relationship to the Father from whom he "proceeds." The Father was always the Father; the Son was always the Son.

Jesus Christ Is One Divine Person

We believe that Jesus Christ is one Person, a divine Person— the Second Person of the Holy Trinity. There are two distinct natures in the one Person of Christ. Jesus has a divine nature and a human nature. He is perfect in divinity and perfect in humanity. Jesus Christ is true God and true man.

> Christ's whole earthly life—his words and deeds, his silences and sufferings, indeed his manner of being and speaking— is *Revelation* of the Father.
>
> ❧
>
> *Catechism of the Catholic Church*, 516

Jesus, God Incarnate, Is Our Savior

We believe that "For us men and for our salvation he came down from heaven" and "For our sake he was crucified under Pontius Pilate; he suffered, died, and was buried. On the third day he rose again in fulfillment of the Scriptures; he ascended into heaven and is seated at the right hand of the Father" (Nicene Creed).

Mary Is Truly the Mother of God

We believe that "by the power of the Holy Spirit he was born of the Virgin Mary, and became man" (Nicene Creed). Mary truly conceived one Person, Jesus Christ, God's only Son become human without giving up his divinity. She is truly the mother (*theotokos,* which means "God-bearer") of the eternal Son of God-made-man, who is God himself.

Because of this unique role Mary was to play in God's plan of salvation, we believe that she was totally preserved from original sin (Immaculate Conception) and remained free from all personal sin throughout her life.

Certain beliefs of our Catholic faith are dogmas of the Church. This means that the Church's teaching on the Incarnation is a true and authentic interpretation of God's revelation to us. It is a belief to which we give the full assent of our mind and heart.

Did You Know?

What does it mean to say we "give full assent of our mind and heart"?

Jesus Christ Is Truly Man

As God-made-man, Jesus has a human intellect and a human will. In Jesus, God truly and fully shared our humanity. The human nature and divine nature in the one Person of Jesus are perfectly united. It is right to say that God truly suffered, died, and rose from the dead for us.

Jesus' Kingdom Will Have No End

If we repent of our sins, believe, and cooperate with the Holy Spirit, we will share in the eternal life he has promised for us. We believe that "He will come again in glory to judge the living and the dead, and his kingdom will have no end" and "We look for the resurrection of the dead, and the life of the world to come. Amen."

(CCC, 512–560)

The Mysteries of Jesus' Life

Everything in Jesus' life on earth is significant. Everything is a sign or revelation of God and God's saving presence in our midst. What this means is that the humanity of Jesus is a sign of his divinity and the salvation he brings. Everything about the life of Jesus, God-made-flesh, reveals the Father and God's loving plan of goodness for all creation.

Jesus launched his public ministry in the "fifteenth year of Tiberius Caesar's reign" (A.D. 27–28) when he was in his thirties. Listed here are some key events of this ministry. Each of these mysteries of the public life of Jesus reveals to us the mystery of God and God's saving love for us.

Baptism of Jesus

The public life or ministry of Jesus was announced at his baptism by John the Baptist, whom God sent to prepare the way. At his baptism the Holy Spirit descended upon Jesus and a heavenly voice proclaimed, "You are my beloved Son; with you I am well pleased" (Mark 1:11). With his baptism, Jesus accepts and launches his mission among us.

Read Matthew 3:13–17.
Why did John want to baptize Jesus?

Temptation in the Desert

In the gospel account of Jesus' temptations in the desert, Jesus repudiates Satan and remains faithful and loyal to God. Jesus is God's obedient servant. This mystery of his life reveals the heart of his mission—ever faithful to God, he will overcome the power of evil and sin in the world and reconcile all creation with God.

Read Luke 4:1–13.
What are the three temptations?

Jesus Preaches God's Kingdom

When he emerged from the desert, Jesus immediately began his preaching ministry. "This is the time of fulfillment. The kingdom of God is at hand. Repent, and believe in the gospel" (Mark 1:15). Jesus and his ministry to bring about the kingdom of God is the "good news." The image "kingdom of God" is used to help us understand the mystery of God's loving plan of goodness for us.

Read Luke, chapter 15.
What is the major point of the parable of the lost coin? The lost sheep? The lost (prodigal) son?

Miracles of Jesus

Jesus did not perform miracles simply to satisfy the curious or to act like a magician. Jesus' miracles were signs of the kingdom of God. The many miracles performed by Jesus call us to faith in God, who lives among us. The miracles of Jesus also invite us to believe in him. They show that Jesus is the Messiah and God's true Son.

Read John, chapter 11.
What does this gospel account reveal about Jesus?

Transfiguration of Jesus

In the mystery of the Transfiguration of Jesus (Matthew 17:1–8, Mark 9:2–13, and Luke 9:28–36), the divine glory of Jesus is revealed. The Transfiguration includes a vision of Moses and Elijah, two Old Testament figures who had seen God's glory on a mountain. Their presence recalls how the revelation given to Israel through Moses and the prophets (Elijah) had announced the sufferings of the Messiah. In this gospel story, the revelation of God as the Holy Trinity is passed on to us. All three Persons of the Trinity appear: the Father in the voice; the Son in Jesus; and the Holy Spirit in the shining cloud.

The Paschal Mystery

The final days of Jesus' life on earth begin with his final journey to the holy

Did You Know?

A heresy is a statement that falsely interprets God's revelation. Here is a list of some of the heresies about Jesus.

Docetism denied that the Son of God really became human. Jesus only appeared to be a man.

Arianism denied the true divinity of Jesus. It taught that God the Father created Jesus as the greatest of creatures, but that Jesus was not equal to God.

Nestorianism taught that Jesus was two persons and that Mary was not really the Mother of God.

Monophysitism held that Christ's divine nature totally absorbed his human nature, destroying Jesus' true humanity.

city of Jerusalem at the time of Passover. Jerusalem, the center of life and worship for the people of the Old Covenant, becomes the place of the new Passover, the New Covenant.

In Jesus, the greatest of God's love for us is revealed. Jesus freely and knowingly sacrifices his life that we might be saved from sin and death. He is raised from the dead and the promise of eternal life is revealed to us. He ascends to heaven to welcome us to live forever in the kingdom of God. Through his Paschal mystery—his passion-death-resurrection-ascension—Christ Jesus, our Lord and Savior, has accomplished once and for all our salvation and fulfills God's loving plan of goodness for us.

We solemnly celebrate and recall the Paschal mystery of Christ each year during the Easter Triduum.

What the Documents Say

The Church teaches us about the mysteries of our faith through the bishops of the world gathered in council with the Pope. The Second Vatican Council taught:

> Jesus Christ was sent into the world as the true Mediator between God and men. Since he is God, all the fullness of the divine nature dwells in him bodily (Colossians 2:9); as man he is the new Adam, full of grace and truth (John 1:14), who has been constituted head of a restored humanity. So the Son of God entered the world by means of a true incarnation that he might make men sharers in the divine nature; though rich, he was made poor for our sake, that by his poverty we might become rich (2 Corinthians 8:9). The Son of man did not come to be served, but to serve and to give his life as a ransom for many, that is, for all (see Mark 10:45).
>
> *Decree on the Church's Missionary Activity, 3*

What truths of our faith are restated in this passage? In particular, how does the description of Jesus "he was made poor for our sake, that by his poverty we might become rich" describe our faith in him?

REVIEW

IMPORTANT TERMS TO KNOW

Christ—a major title for Jesus, meaning "the anointed one." Its derivation comes from the Greek word *christos,* which translates the Hebrew word *messiah.*

dogma—an essential doctrine, or teaching, of the Church issued with the highest authority and solemnity as a truth revealed by God that God's people must believe

evangelist—a proclaimer of the Gospel, the good news of Jesus Christ. "The four evangelists" refers to the authors of the four Gospels: Matthew, Mark, Luke, and John.

Gospel—the term referring to Jesus' preaching of the good news; the good news of salvation, which Jesus Christ won for us (Jesus is the good news the Church proclaims); the four inspired, written accounts of the good news— the Gospels of Matthew, Mark, Luke, and John

heresy—a false teaching that contradicts an essential (dogmatic) teaching of the Church

Incarnation—the dogma that God's eternal Son became man in Jesus Christ, born of the Virgin Mary. (The term literally means "taking on human flesh.")

Paschal mystery—the passion-death-resurrection-ascension of Christ through God's loving plan of salvation

Virgin Mary—the Church dogma that teaches the Virgin Mary conceived and gave birth to Jesus by power of the Holy Spirit, without the cooperation of a human father

CHAPTER SUMMARY

The Incarnation is the mystery of the wonderful union of the divine and human natures in the one person of the Word of God. In this chapter we learned that:

1. Ancient Roman and Jewish writers attest to the existence of Jesus. The New Testament testifies to faith of the Church in Jesus—God's Son become man to reveal God's love, to save and reconcile us with God, and to give us a share in God's own life.

2. The four inspired Gospels came to be written down in a three-stage process: the life of Jesus, oral tradition, and the writing of the Gospels themselves, which were composed between A.D. 65 and A.D. 100.

3. The name *Jesus* means "Savior" or "God saves." The titles of Jesus tell us a great deal about his identity and his ministry: Christ—the Messiah; Lord—God; Son of God—the only Son of the Father; he is God himself; Word of God—substantial image of the Father; Son of Man—one of us, but also God's special heavenly agent.

4. Jesus is the only Son of God, God Incarnate, true God and true man. He is one divine Person with two natures—a divine nature and a human nature.

5. Mary is truly the Mother of God. Our belief in the virgin birth holds that Jesus was conceived by the power of the Holy Spirit and born of the Virgin Mary.

6. The mysteries of Jesus' life reveal to us his identity and ministry.

EXPLORING OUR CATHOLIC FAITH

1. Listening to God's Word

The Gospel according to John was the last of the four canonical Gospels to be written. Read John 1:1–18. What faith beliefs about Jesus are passed on to us in this gospel passage?

2. Understanding the Teachings of the Catholic Church

The Church has come together in councils. Under the guidance of the Holy Spirit these councils teach us the true meaning of God's revelation. Research two of these councils: Nicaea (325), Constantinople 1 (381), Ephesus (431), Chalcedon (451), Constantinople II (553), Constantinople III (680–681), Trent (1545–1563), Vatican I (1869–1870), and Vatican II (1962–1965). What were the main teachings of each council?

3. Reflecting on Our Catholic Faith

Reflect on this insight from a member of our faith community: "Jesus is God spelling himself out in language that humans can understand." How does Jesus "spell out" God for you? How is your life a language that "spells out" God for others? Write your thoughts in your journal.

4. Living Our Catholic Faith

Brainstorm ways the lives of young people "speak" to others about God. Choose one and put it into action.

CHAPTER 4

Jesus Christ, Evangelizer and Savior

"This is my commandment:
love one another as I love you.
No one has greater love than this,
to lay down one's life for one's friends.
You are my friends if you do
what I command you."

JOHN 15:12–14

What Do You Think?

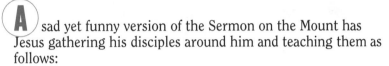

Read and think about the passage from John 15:1–12. In the space provided, list ways you see this commandment being lived in society and ways it is not being lived. Discuss your responses.

Ways the Commandment of Jesus Is Being Lived	Ways the Commandment of Jesus Is Not Being Lived

A sad yet funny version of the Sermon on the Mount has Jesus gathering his disciples around him and teaching them as follows:

❏ "Blessed are the poor in spirit, for theirs is the kingdom of heaven.
❏ Blessed are the meek . . .
❏ Blessed are they who mourn . . .
❏ Blessed are the merciful . . .
❏ Blessed are those who hunger and thirst for righteousness . . .
❏ Blessed are those who are persecuted . . .
❏ Blessed are you when people revile you . . .
❏ Rejoice and be glad, for your reward is great in heaven."

When Jesus is finished, one disciple asks, "Do we have to write this down?

A second asks, "Should we memorize this?"

A third adds, "Will there be a test on this?"

A fourth joins in, "What if we don't understand it?"

A fifth challenges, "This doesn't really have anything to do with real life, does it?"

Then one of the teachers present demands, "Where did you get all these ideas?"

And Jesus wept!

How seriously do we take the teachings of Jesus? Why is that?

KEY TERMS

Abba

kingdom, or reign of God

Parousia

redemption

Resurrection of Christ

salvation

There were probably many times in his teaching career when Jesus felt like crying because people either misunderstood him or his words and his deeds. Still others glibly dismissed him and his teachings and did not even want to take the time to think and figure out the "good news" he preached.

This chapter will examine the teachings of Jesus in a little more depth. It will then explore the meaning of his death and resurrection.

He used similes and taught in short, pithy adages. For example, Jesus said:

> "Amen, I say to you, unless you turn and become like children, you will not enter the kingdom of heaven. Whoever humbles himself like this child is the greatest in the kingdom of heaven. And whoever receives one child such as this in my name receives me."
>
> **Matthew 18:3–5**

(Catechism of the Catholic Church, 541–553)

Jesus the Evangelizer Jesus, Proclaimer of the Good News

Jesus is the preeminent evangelizer—that is, proclaimer of the good news. The heart of his message was that God's kingdom was coming in Jesus' very person. This requires a response—repentance and faith in him. Jesus delivered his message with deep conviction, enthusiasm, and unique authority. He was a teacher who was beyond compare.

Jesus the Teacher

Jesus taught his message in a variety of ways. **First,** he used spoken language. He delivered short, revolutionary discourses like the Sermon on the Mount. He taught in parables, vivid and memorable short stories that drove home earthshaking lessons. For example, the parable of the Good Samaritan emphatically teaches we must love everyone, even our enemies.

Second, Jesus the Evangelizer taught his message by the way he treated people who were poor, needy, suffering, or sick. He, to the amazement of onlookers, treated women, foreigners, children, sinners, and his enemies with equal respect and love—the respect and love of God for all.

His words and actions—his values in action—often went against some of the values promoted by the religious, social, and political groups of his day. Consider the time he ate with the notorious tax collector, Zacchaeus. Jesus' opponents "began to grumble, saying, 'He has gone to stay at the house of a sinner' " (Luke 19:7).

Third, the most dramatic and important revelation and proclamation of the good news is the Paschal mystery, that is, the passion-death-resurrection-glorification of Jesus Christ. Through this mystery of divine love, we learn that Jesus is the way to **salvation** and eternal life. We are invited to join ourselves to Jesus by the power of the Holy Spirit. Jesus taught, "Whoever loves me will keep my word, and my Father will love him, and we will come to him and make our dwelling with him" (John 14:23).

Everything about Jesus—God Incarnate—communicated the good news of the fulfillment of God's loving plan of goodness for all. Everything about Jesus reveals God is merciful and loving and lives in our midst.

The Good News of God's Kingdom

This is a short summary of the main points of Jesus' proclamation of the good news.

God's kingdom is here. Jesus announced and began the building of the reign, or kingdom, of God. His works of healing—especially his Paschal mystery—are the principal signs of the kingdom. They reveal God's power and saving activity in the entire universe—in heaven and on earth. We also work to bring about that kingdom when we cooperate with the Spirit in works of love, forgiveness, healing, compassion, and justice that bring about true righteousness and peace.

Jesus taught that the kingdom's presence might appear small now and that the forces of evil will resist it, but its growth is inevitable. It is comparable to the mustard seed—the tiniest of seeds that grows to be among the largest of plants. When the kingdom finally comes about and when Christ returns in glory, all of humanity will be transformed.

The Church is the seed of the kingdom. Christ is the head of the Church, the Body of Christ. He is the vine; we are the branches. He is always with us. The Lord himself wants us to share in his work of proclaiming and living as signs of the kingdom. The payoff is great—a life of eternal happiness with our loving, Triune God.

God's merciful love is the principal sign of the kingdom. God is love and mercy. God's love and mercy are extended to everyone—without exception. God's love reveals itself in his Son, God Incarnate, who came to live with and die for us. Jesus reached out to his Father with simple childlike confidence and trust; we are invited to do the same. God is like—but incredibly more loving, more forgiving, more merciful, more welcoming than—the father of the prodigal son (Luke 15:11–32).

We are to live as images of our merciful, loving, and compassionate Father. Jesus, our Lord and Savior, is the very image of the compassionate God. "The Father and I are one" (John 10:30). By our baptism we become members of the Body of Christ, the Church. We are his disciples— the "salt of the earth" and the "light of the world."

To accept Jesus and his message means to commit ourselves to Jesus and live a moral and loving life of serving others. This is tough to do, especially in a world that glorifies pleasure. We must turn our backs on sin and refuse to base our lives on false values that lead us to an "empty" happiness. A Christian life requires living a life of self-denial and sacrifice.

Then Jesus said to his disciples, "Whoever wishes to come after me must deny himself, take up his cross, and follow me. For whoever wishes to save his life will lose it, but whoever loses his life for my sake will find it."

Matthew 16:24–25

The Holy Spirit is our Guide and Teacher. Jesus and his Father have sent us the Holy Spirit to empower us to live as his disciples. We receive the

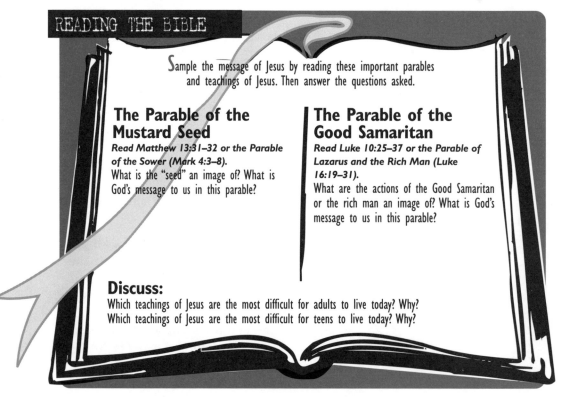

READING THE BIBLE

Sample the message of Jesus by reading these important parables and teachings of Jesus. Then answer the questions asked.

The Parable of the Mustard Seed
Read Matthew 13:31–32 or the Parable of the Sower (Mark 4:3–8).
What is the "seed" an image of? What is God's message to us in this parable?

The Parable of the Good Samaritan
Read Luke 10:25–37 or the Parable of Lazarus and the Rich Man (Luke 16:19–31).
What are the actions of the Good Samaritan or the rich man an image of? What is God's message to us in this parable?

Discuss:
Which teachings of Jesus are the most difficult for adults to live today? Why?
Which teachings of Jesus are the most difficult for teens to live today? Why?

Spirit of Christ, who guides us in living as other Christians and in continuing his mission of spreading the good news. The gift of the Holy Spirit empowers us, the Body of Christ, with many gifts that guide us in living a Christian life. As members of the Church, which is the Temple of the Holy Spirit, we continue to preach and exemplify God's kingdom.

(CCC, 456–463, 599–623)

Jesus the Savior

Jesus spent three years preaching the good news of salvation, relieving the suffering of others. However, he himself did not avoid suffering and death. Jesus' whole reason for coming to us clarifies itself in his passion, death, and resurrection. Through this Paschal mystery of God's love, Jesus reconciles humanity to God, heals our brokenness, and renews everything.

The Name Jesus

At the time Joseph learned that Mary was to become the mother of God's Son, the angel told Joseph, "[Y]ou are to name him Jesus, because he will save his people from their sins" (Matthew 1:21). This is a very important element in the gospel story of Jesus' birth. For the writers of the Gospels, a person's name is a revelation of that person's identity— of their life's work. By showing that the child of Mary is to be called Jesus, the writer of Matthew's gospel story is professing the faith of the early Church that Jesus is indeed the Savior of the world, promised by God.

Jesus came to bring us salvation. Salvation flows from God's initiative of love for us. Because he loves us, God sent his Son to be the expiation for our sins. The salvation that Jesus brings repairs our broken relationship with God and others. Salvation bestows God's blessings, grace, and life on us and adopts us into God's family as his beloved children. Jesus' gift of salvation forgives our sins and redeems us from sin, evil, and death.

Jesus alone brings salvation. He is the only Savior. As Peter proclaimed, "There is no salvation through anyone else, nor is there any other name under heaven given to the human race by which we are to be saved" (Acts 4:12). His life and love, his service and sacrifice, and especially his death-resurrection have won for us the forgiveness of sin and eternal life.

The Suffering and Death of Jesus

At the beginning of John's gospel story, John the Baptist identifies Jesus, saying, "Behold, the Lamb of God, who takes away the sin of the world" (John 1:29). In the Old Testament the lamb is most often mentioned in ritual passage as the victim of sacrifice. And at the time of Passover, the meal is celebrated with the Passover lamb.

The identification of Jesus as the "Lamb of God" is clearly a statement of the apostolic faith that Jesus is the new Passover lamb who sacrificed his life for us. The New Testament explains that Jesus' death is a **"redemption"** (Romans 3:24) and a sacrifice of atonement (Romans 3:25), and that he will "give his life as a ransom for many" (Mark 10:45).

Jesus' death was for all humans for all times. Jesus, the Suffering Servant, took our sins to the cross and freely gave his all for us. The life he freely surrendered became both the perfect offering and the instrument of God's love, a gift that opened eternal life to us. His obedient acceptance of suffering and death restored to the Father a new humanity.

Jesus freely offered his life to liberate us from our sins and to bestow eternal life on us. He underwent the excruciating torments of the most painful form of death devised by human beings out of his immense love for us. By doing so, he has given us the hope of eternal life—a life where there will be no suffering or death.

The Resurrection and Ascension

Jesus' death was real. It is truly the Son of God made man who died and was buried. Sin's greatest result is death. Jesus allowed death to touch him. He really experienced a separation of his soul from his body between the time of his death and his **resurrection.** This was the price of our salvation and a real proof that his resurrection truly conquered sin and death.

Jesus Died, Was Buried, and Descended to the Dead

Joseph of Arimathea, a member of the Sanhedrin, buried Jesus. Nicodemus, the Blessed Mother, and Mary Magdalene witnessed this burial, a sign that Jesus was truly dead. Matthew's Gospel even tells us that the Jewish authorities had a guard posted at the tomb for fear that someone would steal Jesus' corpse.

In the Apostles' Creed we profess that Christ "descended into hell," which means that he went to the abode of the dead (*Sheol* in Hebrew, *Hades* in Greek) to proclaim the good news to the just who had died. Then, on the first day of the week, he rose from the dead, appearing to his disciples.

Jesus Rose from the Dead!

The Gospels and Apostolic Tradition clearly pass on to us that the apostles encountered the Risen One after his death and burial. Hiding in fear in an upper room in Jerusalem, the apostles at first refused to believe the women who reported that they had seen an empty tomb and the Risen Lord alive. Returning to the empty tomb was their first step toward believing that the Father brought his Son back to life.

The apostles and disciples believed when they actually saw the Risen Lord. Paul reports in 1 Corinthians 15:5–8

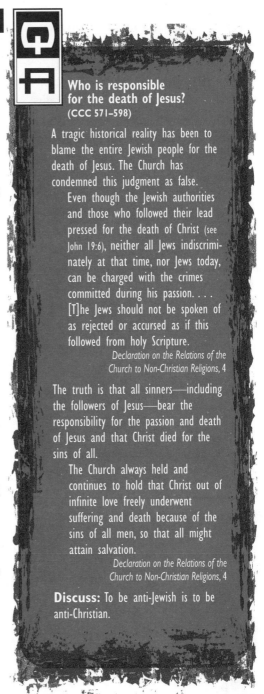

Who is responsible for the death of Jesus?
(CCC 571–598)

A tragic historical reality has been to blame the entire Jewish people for the death of Jesus. The Church has condemned this judgment as false.
Even though the Jewish authorities and those who followed their lead pressed for the death of Christ (see John 19:6), neither all Jews indiscriminately at that time, nor Jews today, can be charged with the crimes committed during his passion. . . . [T]he Jews should not be spoken of as rejected or accursed as if this followed from holy Scripture.
Declaration on the Relations of the Church to Non-Christian Religions, 4

The truth is that all sinners—including the followers of Jesus—bear the responsibility for the passion and death of Jesus and that Christ died for the sins of all.
The Church always held and continues to hold that Christ out of infinite love freely underwent suffering and death because of the sins of all men, so that all might attain salvation.
Declaration on the Relations of the Church to Non-Christian Religions, 4

Discuss: To be anti-Jewish is to be anti-Christian.

that Jesus appeared to many witnesses. These witnesses included:

❏ Simon Peter and the other apostles; more than five hundred men and women, many of whom were still alive in the 50s, when Paul was writing;

❏ James, the leader of the Jerusalem church;

❏ and Paul himself at a time when he was still persecuting the Christians.

These actual encounters with the Risen Lord completely changed the frightened, confused, and bitterly disappointed followers of the crucified Jesus. They were transformed into bold witnesses who testified that "Jesus is Lord!"

Jesus' resurrection is at the heart of our Christian faith. Saint Paul wrote to Christians living in Corinth:

> If there is no resurrection of the dead, then neither has Christ been raised. And if Christ has not been raised, then empty [too] is our preaching; empty, too, your faith.
>
> **1 Corinthians 15:13–14**

When the Lord rose from the dead, death died! Our salvation is real. The Author of Life destroyed the power of the Evil One (whom Scripture names the Devil, Satan). Christ has freed us from death and opened the gates of heaven and eternal life to us.

The Nature of the Resurrection

When we profess our faith in the resurrection of Christ, we are professing that the Risen Lord was truly alive in a new and transformed way. His human body was gloriously transfigured, fully pervaded with God's Holy Spirit, into an incorrupt, glorious, immortal body "seated at the right hand of the Father."

At the Resurrection Jesus did not receive a reanimated corpse—a body like that of Lazarus—come back to life that would die again. It was not simply a way of saying that only Jesus' soul was immortal and not his body, a belief held by early heretics. It was not reincarnation, which holds that our souls are reborn successively into a series of

READING THE BIBLE

Read John 20:1–29 to see how one of the evangelists reports the resurrection of Jesus. Then answer each question in the space provided.

To whom does Jesus first appear? What mission does Jesus give the apostles when he first appears to them?

What does Thomas proclaim when he first sees Jesus?

new bodies. Finally, the Resurrection was not a psychological creation of the apostles who were simply trying to say that they now believed in the cause of their dead master. All these are false interpretations of the Resurrection.

The Meaning of the Resurrection

The Resurrection attests to the truth of Jesus' claims and his mission among us. Raised to a glorious body and filled with the power of the Holy Spirit, our Lord has definitively conquered sin and death. Jesus is indeed Lord. The Risen Christ, the incarnate Son in whom the Father is well pleased, returns to the loving communion of the Father and the Holy Spirit. Christ, the first-born of the dead, is the principle of our own resurrection.

Jesus' death-resurrection repairs our friendship with God. It "atones" for our sins and makes us "one" with God. It frees us from slavery to sin, death, and suffering. Jesus' resurrection gives us hope for eternal life. As Paul assures the early Christians living in Rome:

> [I]f you confess with your mouth that Jesus is Lord and believe in your heart that God raised him from the dead, you will be saved.
> **Romans 10:9**

We profess that same faith today:

In him, who rose from the dead,
our hope of resurrection dawned.
The sadness of death gives way
to the bright promise of immortality.

Lord, for your faithful people
life is changed, not ended.
When the body of our earthly
dwelling lies in death
we gain an everlasting dwelling
place in heaven. Preface, Christian Death I

Through the Sacraments of Initiation (Baptism, Confirmation, and Eucharist), we become members of the Body of Christ. Through water and the Spirit we share in and become witnesses to the suffering-death-resurrection of Christ. In memory of his death and resurrection, we join at Eucharist and unite ourselves with Christ and the Holy Spirit and give praise and thanks to the Father. We share in the Body and Blood of Christ and are strengthened to "go in peace to love and serve the Lord."

Because of our faith in the Resurrection, we profess that the Risen Lord is with us. He himself remains with his Church, especially through the sacraments. He continues to lead us through teachers he appointed to guide us in his truth. The Lord meets us in each other and, in a special way, in the least of those in our midst. The Lord himself tells us that we meet him in people who are hungry or thirsty, in people who are homeless and needy, in people who are sick or in prison (see Matthew 25:31–45). The King of the Universe is not a distant king. He is actively and spiritually present in believers and in the world in which we live. We await the day when he will come in all his glory.

(CCC, 668–682)

Jesus Will Come Again!

Christ's ascension marks his definitive entrance of Jesus' humanity into God's heavenly domain. No longer limited by space and time, our Lord lives and reigns forever. We profess:

He ascended into heaven
and is seated at the right hand of the
  Father.
He will come again to judge
the living and the dead. Apostles' Creed

Both the Apostles' Creed and the Nicene Creed proclaim with great confidence the **Parousia**—the arrival of Jesus in all his glory and his second coming. When this happens, the world as we know it will end. All creatures in the universe will recognize and acknowledge Jesus' Lordship. Jesus will fully establish the Father's kingdom of justice, love, and peace. However, we do not know when this part of the mystery of God's loving plan for us will take place. Its "hour" is hidden. "But of that day or hour, no one knows, neither the angels in heaven, nor the Son, but only the Father" (Mark 13:32). But we believe it will come about. "Be watchful! Be alert!" Jesus tells us. "You do not know when the time will come. . . . What I say to you, I say to all: 'Watch!' " (Mark 13:33, 37)

On this day Jesus will come to judge the living and the dead. Matthew, chapter 25, provides the criteria for his judgment. Did we feed the hungry and give drink to the thirsty? Were we hospitable to strangers? Did we respond to the poor, the sick, the imprisoned? In other words, did we love Jesus by loving our neighbor?

Jesus in My Life

Discuss: If you thought you would meet Christ tonight at midnight, what *three* things would you do today to prepare for this meeting? Why did you choose these?

REVIEW

IMPORTANT TERMS TO KNOW

ascension of Jesus—the return of the Risen Lord to his Father

kingdom, or reign, of God—the saving power and presence of God that reconciles and renews everything through the Son; the kingdom takes root when God's will is done on earth as it is in heaven, a process begun with Jesus that will be completed perfectly at the end of time

Parousia—the second coming of Christ at the end of time, when the Lord will judge the living and the dead. At the Parousia, God's kingdom (or reign) will be fully established.

redemption—the activity of God through Christ in saving humankind from sin and evil; the word means "buying back"

Resurrection of Christ—the raising of Jesus from the dead

salvation—the healing and deliverance from sin whereby God's forgiveness, grace, and reconciliation are extended to us through Jesus Christ in the Holy Spirit. Salvation brings about union with God and with our fellow humans through the life-death-resurrection-ascension of Jesus Christ.

CHAPTER SUMMARY

In faith, we know who Jesus really is and what he has done for us. In this chapter we learned that:

1. Jesus announced and brought about through his words and actions the kingdom of God. The principal sign of God's kingdom is his limitless mercy and compassion, his forgiveness of everyone, saints and sinners alike.

2. Jesus Christ is the one and only Savior who brought us salvation. He is the one who reconciles us with God and each other. Jesus is our Savior, principally through the Paschal mystery of his passion-death-resurrection-glorification. Jesus was obedient to his Father and freely chose to sacrifice his life for us, to redeem us, and to allow us to participate in God's own life.

3. Jesus not only freed us from sin and death but brought us eternal life.

4. Jesus died a real death. He was buried in a known tomb. He descended into hell and proclaimed the good news of salvation to the righteous ones abiding there.

5. Jesus' resurrection is the basis of our Christian faith. Jesus really rose from the dead, and the Risen Lord appeared to many who attest to the fact of his resurrection.

6. At the Parousia, Christ will come again in glory to establish God's kingdom fully and to judge the living and the dead.

7. Jesus promised he would always remain with us by power of the Holy Spirit. We meet Christ today through the Church, the sacraments and prayer, the proclamation and reading of the Scriptures, and through each other—especially the "least" of our brothers and sisters.

EXPLORING OUR CATHOLIC FAITH

1. Listening to God's Word

The passing on of the Paschal mystery is at the heart of the Gospel. Read Mark 14:43–15:47. What does Mark's Gospel tell about Jesus' arrest, trial, suffering, death, burial, and resurrection? List the important details you may have forgotten that reading Mark's account helped you recall.

2. Understanding the Teachings of the Catholic Church

In the *Catechism of the Catholic Church*, we read, "Christ's Resurrection is closely linked to the Incarnation of God's Son and is its fulfillment in accordance with God's eternal plan" (653). Discuss your understanding of this statement with another person.

3. Reflecting on Our Catholic Faith

Reflect on this statement: "If, then, you are looking for the way by which you should go, take Christ, because he himself is the way." In what ways does this insight into Christian living help you live as a follower of Christ? Write your reflections in your journal.

4. Living Our Catholic Faith

How well are you at putting the teachings of Jesus into practice? Read and think about these teachings: accept others (Matthew 7:1); self-denial (Luke 9:23); love (Matthew 7:12); seek first the kingdom (Matthew 6:33–34); simplicity in living (Luke 12:15); prayer (Matthew 7:7). How is each teaching part of your life?

CHAPTER 5

The Holy Spirit: The Love of God

When the time for Pentecost was fulfilled, they were all in one place together. And suddenly there came from the sky a noise like a strong driving wind, and it filled the entire house in which they were. Then there appeared to them tongues as of fire, which parted and came to rest on each one of them. And they were all filled with the holy Spirit and began to speak in different tongues, as the Spirit enabled them to proclaim.

ACTS 2:1–4

What Do You Think?

Complete these statements. Discuss your responses.

1. The most important effect of the Holy Spirit coming on Pentecost Sunday was

2. The images of fire and wind are used by the Scripture writers to help us understand the Holy Spirit. These images tell us

3. Some of the teachings of the Catholic Church regarding the Holy Spirit are

Some friends were on a school trip to Niagara Falls—one of the great wonders of the natural world. As their bus traveled along the thundering Niagara River, they were in awe of the roaring power of the rapids right before the falls and the peaceful mist rising in a rainbow of colors from the rocks below.

"There's the greatest unused power in the world!" one student remarked.

"I agree," answered another student. "But there is a greater unused power within each of us. That power is the Holy Spirit of the living God."

Imagine you are an apostle gathered in the upper room of a disciple's home in Jerusalem. You experience the power of the Holy Spirit descending upon you in the form of a mighty heavenly wind and in the form of tongues of fire. Describe your faith prior to the coming of the Spirit. Then describe your faith as the Spirit comes upon you as Jesus had promised.

KEY TERMS

Advocate

charism

fruits of the Holy Spirit

gifts of the Holy Spirit

grace

Holy Spirit

Paraclete

How right the student is! For many, the Holy Spirit is the most mysterious of the three Persons of the Holy Trinity. The Spirit's effect on our lives as Christians is profound. Without the Spirit's awesome power and magnificent gifts, we would be powerless to live the Christian life. In this chapter we will examine the Church's teaching about the **Holy Spirit**—the Spirit of love who energizes us to live as courageous followers of Jesus Christ.

(Catechism of the Catholic Church, 683–701, 731–741, 1829–1832)

The Coming of the Spirit

The effects of the Spirit's coming upon the disciples were awesome. The disciples were no longer fearful, questioning, or uncertain about Jesus or his meaning.

Pentecost

The apostles left the upper room and went into the streets of the city of Jerusalem. They fearlessly preached. Their enthusiasm attracted many; at the same time, it made others skeptical. Some even thought the zealousness of the apostles was a sign that they were drunk. What was taking place in their midst, Peter assured them, was the fulfillment of Joel's prophecy:

> "It will come to pass in the last days," God says,
> "that I will pour out a portion of my spirit upon all flesh." **Acts 2:17**

Peter assured his audience that God had kept his promises by working marvelously through Jesus of Nazareth. This Jesus—who had taught in their midst, who had worked miracles, who had been crucified—now lives! God raised Jesus from the dead. Jesus of Nazareth is the promised Messiah. He is Lord and now exalted at God's right hand!

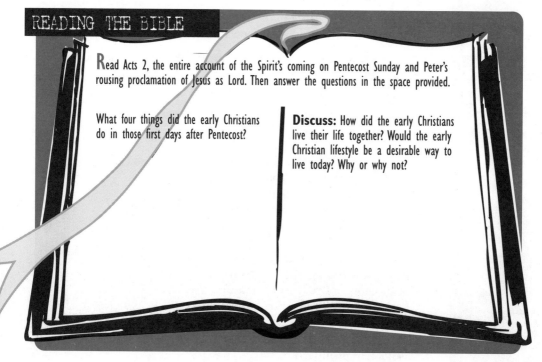

READING THE BIBLE

Read Acts 2, the entire account of the Spirit's coming on Pentecost Sunday and Peter's rousing proclamation of Jesus as Lord. Then answer the questions in the space provided.

What four things did the early Christians do in those first days after Pentecost?

Discuss: How did the early Christians live their life together? Would the early Christian lifestyle be a desirable way to live today? Why or why not?

We have witnessed all of this, continued Peter. What the people must do, he concluded, was to "[r]epent and be baptized, every one of you, in the name of Jesus Christ for the forgiveness of your sins; and you will receive the gift of the holy Spirit" (Acts 2:38).

The Spirit's power remained with the apostles as they continued to preach, baptize, and heal in Jesus' name. By the end of the apostolic era, they had preached to every corner of the Roman Empire until eventually Peter and Paul made their way to Rome. This same Spirit continues to give life to the Church and is powerfully active in the world today, continuing Christ's work of salvation in every corner of the globe.

The Holy Spirit at Work in the Church and in the World

We celebrate Pentecost as the birthday of the Church. On that day we celebrate and remember that Jesus' promise was fulfilled. The Spirit came and dwells among us as our **Paraclete** and **Advocate,** our Helper and Giver of Life. With the Spirit's coming, the Paschal mystery finds its completion and the mystery of the Holy Trinity is fully revealed. The Holy Spirit creates and sustains the Church.

The Holy Spirit is indispensable for Christian life. He enables us to profess that Jesus is the Lord and to call God "Father." Through baptism, the Holy Spirit comes to us, we receive the gift of faith, we are reborn of water and the Spirit as adopted children of God.

The Holy Spirit is at work in the Church today in many ways. He is present in:

❏ the Scriptures,
❏ Sacred Tradition,

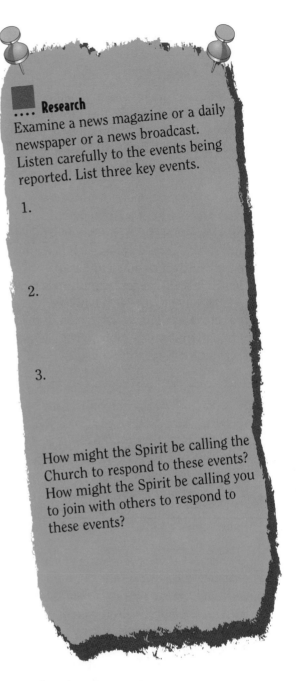

Research

Examine a news magazine or a daily newspaper or a news broadcast. Listen carefully to the events being reported. List three key events.

1.

2.

3.

How might the Spirit be calling the Church to respond to these events? How might the Spirit be calling you to join with others to respond to these events?

❏ the Church's Magisterium,
❏ the sacraments,
❏ the various gifts and ministries that build up the Church,
❏ the signs associated with the apostolic and missionary life of the Church, and
❏ the witness of the saints throughout the ages.

Images and Names for the Holy Spirit

Sacred Scripture uses many images and titles for the Spirit of God. These help us understand the mystery of who the Spirit is and the Spirit's work among us.

Holy Spirit is the name Jesus gave as the correct form of address for the third Person of the Holy Trinity. "Holy" and "spirit" are attributes each Person of the Trinity have in common. However, the Bible and the Church's theological and liturgical language indicate the unique third Person of the Blessed Trinity—the Holy Spirit—when they use them together.

Spirit—The term *Spirit* translates the Hebrew word *ruah,* which means "breath," "air," "wind," and "soul." The Old Testament uses *ruah* 379 times to describe God's activities. Psalm 18:11 compares God's power and mystery to *wind.* Ezekiel 37 speaks of the *breath* of God giving life; without God's Spirit there is only death.

At creation, God's *ruah* hovers over the chaotic waters (Genesis 1:1–2:4). Along with God's word, his Spirit brings forth light, order, and life. In the second creation story of Genesis (2:4–25), God *breathes life* into Adam, whom he formed from clay. The breath of life—God's spirit in us—gives us the ability to live as humans, to communicate with and love God.

Paul and Peter continue to speak fervently of the life-giving Holy Spirit when they refer to the "Spirit of Christ," the "Spirit of adoption," the "Spirit of the Lord," the "Spirit of God," and the "Spirit of glory."

"And I will ask the Father, and he will give you another Advocate to be with you always."
John 14:16

Paraclete—When Jesus was nearing the end of his earthly ministry, he promised to send a Paraclete, that is, an Advocate, a Consoler, a Helper. This Helper is the Spirit of truth who will "guide you to all truth. He will not speak on his own, but he will speak what he hears, and will declare to you the things that are coming" (John 16:13).

Besides *spirit, wind,* and *breath,* the Bible uses many other rich images to describe the Holy Spirit. Here are some.

Fire—Yahweh revealed himself to Moses in a burning bush. As pillars of fire, he led the Israelites through the desert. Fire purifies and transforms. It is life-giving, making one holy. It also destroys, as when God rained down fire on the wicked in Sodom.

Light—Jesus is the light of the world. He taught that we were to be light. He gave us the Spirit—the power and energy to enlighten the world—to help us burn with the love of God.

Tongues of Fire—The tongue is the organ of speech, the vehicle of truth. Jesus was filled with the truth of God the Father. His words proclaimed the forgiveness of sin, brought about healing, commanded nature to obey, and revealed power over death by raising the dead. The Holy Spirit enables us to preach Jesus in truth and helps us form community in his name.

In the Old Testament, a dove (actually a bird from the pigeon family) released by Noah returned with an olive branch to show that the flood waters were receding. This symbol of life also appears as a purification offering for the poor (Leviticus 5:7). In the New Testament all four Gospels report that the Spirit descended on Jesus at his baptism in the form of a dove. The dove recalls God's presence hovering over the water at creation and points to God's Spirit present uniquely in his Son at Jesus' baptism. The dove is also a symbol of purity, innocence, gentleness, peace, and virtue—all fruits of union with the Holy Spirit.

Your Own Image for the Spirit

Reflect on the presence of the Holy Spirit in your life. In what ways is the Spirit your advocate? In what ways is the Spirit your helper and guide?

In this space, create your own image of the Holy Spirit. Write a brief explanation of your image.

Explanation:

Water—Water represents both death and life. At the time of Noah, water was the source of the destruction of humanity caught in sin. On the other hand, water represented life to the Israelites wandering in the desert. Jesus taught that rebirth in the waters of baptism and the Holy Spirit is a requirement of salvation: "Amen, amen, I say to you, no one can enter the kingdom of God without being born of water and Spirit" (John 3:5).

Spiritual regeneration through water and the Spirit in baptism turns us from a life of sin to the eternal life promised us. It is the Holy Spirit who accomplishes this for us, initiating us into God's family.

Hand—Several sacraments (for example, Confirmation and Holy Orders) deepen the giving of the Holy Spirit through the laying on of hands. This recalls the power of the Spirit unleashed when Jesus healed through touch, a power he also gave to his apostles.

The Gift of God

When the Father and the Son send the Spirit to us, they are giving us the incredible gift of God himself to live in us. The Holy Spirit is God's **grace** to us. *Grace* means "good will" or "gift given." The gift of the Spirit is the gift of God, the gift of love which fills our hearts. John writes, "God is love, and whoever remains in love remains in God and God in him" (1 John 4:16).

By virtue of our baptism, we receive the gift of the Spirit. We become living temples of the Holy Spirit. This gift of the Holy Spirit—God dwelling within us—brings us life-giving benefits.

Forgiveness of Sins

The first major effect of the gift of God's love, the Holy Spirit, is our justification before God, that is, the forgiving of our sins. This forgiveness restores the divine image in us that sin has wounded. Second, and most important, the Holy Spirit transforms us from slaves to adopted children of an incredibly loving God. Paul states it so well when he writes:

For you did not receive a spirit of slavery to fall back into fear, but you received a spirit of adoption, through which we cry, "Abba, Father!" The Spirit itself bears witness with our spirit that we are children of God, and if children, then heirs, heirs of God and joint heirs with Christ, if only we suffer with him so that we may also be glorified with him.

Romans 8:15–17

Life as Children of God

Because God lives in us, we are children of God. We are now able to love in imitation of God's love. We can truly live as children of the light and participate in Christ's eternal life because we have the gift of God loving in and through us.

This last point emphasizes the truth that it is the Holy Spirit who builds, animates, and makes holy the Church, the Body of Christ. The Spirit draws us to and teaches us about Christ. Moreover, the Spirit makes Christ's Paschal mystery present in the Church through the sacraments, especially through the Eucharist.

The Church must, for our part, live as children of God, the Body of Christ, and the Temple of the Holy Spirit. We must announce, make present, and spread love, that is, the mystery of the Holy Trinity.

The Giver of Life

In addition to this central and all-important gift of love, the Holy Spirit showers us with many other gifts to help us live as God's children. These unmerited gifts are not for our self-glorification but for building up the Body of Christ, the Church. These include:

Gifts that build up the Church. These are **charisms,** or special gifts, that are given for the benefit of the church community, not for the individual. These name ways that God is actively present in the community. Paul lists them in his First Letter to the Corinthians. They are wisdom, knowledge, faith, healing, miracle-working, prophecy, discernment, speaking in tongues, and interpreting tongues (1 Corinthians 12:4–11).

Gifts that give spiritual fruit. Paul also describes certain **fruits of the Holy Spirit,** or perfections, that result from the Holy Spirit living in us. These fruits are the first signs of eternal glory working in us. They are love, joy, peace, patience, kindness, generosity, faithfulness, gentleness, and self-control (Galatians 5:16–25).

Gifts that sanctify. The seven **gifts of the Holy Spirit** incline us to the promptings of the Spirit. These gifts are wisdom, understanding, knowledge, counsel, fortitude, piety, and fear of the Lord.

(CCC, 103–108, 702–730)

The Holy Spirit in Salvation History

Before the coming of Christ and the descent of the Holy Spirit, the joint mission of the Father's Word and Spirit were at work—but hidden. Today, the Church can search through the Old Testament and discover in its Spirit-inspired prayers, sacred histories, maxims, and other writings—the gradual unfolding of divine revelation about Christ. This is possible because the Holy Spirit had "spoken through the prophets," that is, he had inspired the authors of the sacred Hebrew Scriptures who used their literary abilities to write what God wanted written for our benefit.

We look on the Bible as a rich source of the Spirit's instruction, not only about salvation history but for guiding our lives. When we read, meditate on, and live the Sacred Scriptures, we are responding to the Holy Spirit, who continues to teach us today. He also enlightens the pope and bishops when

Gifts of the Spirit Coat of Arms

Fill in the coat of arms below to describe the ways the Spirit's gifts are active in your life. Then share with one other person several of your responses.

WISDOM (ability to look at reality from God's point of view)

What is the best quality God sees in you?

COUNSEL (right judgment—helps us form our conscience in light of church teaching)

Mention a time you knew something was right, even though your friends thought otherwise.

UNDERSTANDING (helps us reflect on the deeper meaning of our faith)

What aspect of our faith do you wish to learn more about?

FORTITUDE (gives us the strength to do the right thing)

Give an example of when you had the courage to do right.

KNOWLEDGE (enables us to have a more complete grasp of our faith and the way in which God reveals himself in this world)

Note a time God was with you in a special way.

PIETY (reverence of the Lord and respect for the dignity of others)

Note a time you defended another who was being unfairly attacked.

FEAR OF THE LORD (shows concern about the reality of sin in one's life)

What character trait must you work on to get closer to God?

they instruct us on the meaning of the Bible and its application to daily life.

Here is a brief overview of how the Spirit was actively involved in salvation history.

❏ **At creation** The Breath (*ruah*) of God and the Word of God were at work in the creation of everything that exists, especially breathing life into Adam and Eve, made in God's image and likeness.

❏ **In the covenant with Abraham** Faith and the power of the Spirit were very much at work in Abraham fathering a child. From his progeny the Messiah would come, filled with the Spirit.

❏ **In the manifestations of God and the Law** The Holy Spirit was present in the cloud and fire when Yahweh called Moses and gave the Law. It was the power of God's Spirit that enabled the Chosen People to observe the Law.

❏ **In the kingdom and the Exile** The Spirit inspired kings like David who would rule in Yahweh's name. But the Israelites forgot the Law and were unfaithful to the Covenant. Eventually they were carried off to exile, where the Spirit sustained them until they could return to the Promised Land. During many years of infidelity and exile, the Spirit spoke through the prophets, who called people to fidelity and promised repeatedly the coming of a new king, a servant-messiah. On this person, God's Spirit would rest in a unique way.

❏ **Especially in the ministry and person of Jesus Christ** Jesus did not abolish the Law of Sinai, but rather fulfilled it with such perfection that he revealed its ultimate meaning. In the fullness of time, the Holy Spirit completed in Mary all

Q: Is the Holy Spirit God?
(CCC, 243–248, 689–690)

A: The Holy Spirit is neither a spiritual creature, like an angel, nor an impersonal force. The Holy Spirit is God. He is the "giver of life," whose primary mission is adoption into the divine family, uniting us to Christ Jesus so he can live in us. By uniting us to the Son, we are united with the Father.

The Holy Spirit not only bestows God's life on us but also teaches, guides, and fortifies the Body of Christ—individual Christians and also the leaders of the Church. As our interior Teacher, the Spirit enables us to be followers of Christ. Paul writes, "And no one can say, 'Jesus is Lord,' except by the holy Spirit" (1 Corinthians 12:3).

the preparations for Christ's coming among the people of God. By the action of the Holy Spirit in her, the Father gives the world Emmanuel, "God-with-us." The Spirit's power enabled Mary to conceive the Messiah. She, a humble servant, full of God's grace, was used by the Holy Spirit as a means to bring people into communion again with God.

The Spirit spoke through John the Baptist, the precursor of the Lord and a great prophet who prepared people for the way of the Lord. The Spirit anointed Jesus at his baptism, led him into the desert, and empowered him to preach the Gospel in Nazareth and the surrounding villages. The Spirit worked marvelous deeds through Jesus. He anointed Jesus to preach the good news to the afflicted, to proclaim liberty to captives, to give sight to the blind, and to free the oppressed (see Luke 4:16–21). Jesus testified often to the Holy Spirit during his ministry, demonstrating in fact that his work was a joint mission of the Son and the Holy Spirit.

Jesus gradually revealed the mystery of the Holy Spirit, as in his teaching to Nicodemus about rebirth in the Spirit, to the Samaritan woman at the well, and to the crowds when he taught about the Eucharist.

The Spirit remained with Jesus throughout his ministry, even to his death when the soldier stabbed him with a spear. This wound caused blood and water to gush, symbolizing the life and waters of the Holy Spirit flowing out to the whole world. Through the Holy Spirit, God the Father raised Jesus, who took on a glorified, spiritual body. Through the power of the Holy Spirit, Jesus remains with the Church as its invisible head. As we will see later, the Holy Spirit is the soul of the Church, giving it life and guiding it in Christ's

The Holy Spirit in Your Life

Read Luke 4:14–30 and answer these questions.

What was Jesus proclaiming about the Scripture passage he had read?

How did the people react to Jesus' claim?

In what ways is the Spirit present with you?

What is the Spirit calling you to do?

How do people react to you when you do the work of the Spirit?

REVIEW

IMPORTANT TERMS TO KNOW

Advocate—title for Holy Spirit; means "helper, consoler"

charism—a special gift of the Holy Spirit that helps us build up the Church, the Body of Christ. Examples include the ability to express wisdom and knowledge, healing, prophecy, and discernment of spirits. (See 1 Corinthians 12:4–11.)

fruits of the Holy Spirit—perfections that result from living a life in the Holy Spirit. They include love, joy, peace, patience, kindness, generosity, faithfulness, gentleness, and self-control. (See Galatians 5:22–23.)

gifts of the Holy Spirit—Spirit-given abilities that help us live a Christian life. Jesus bestows these gifts on us through the Holy Spirit. They are wisdom, understanding, knowledge, counsel (right judgment), fortitude (courage), piety (reverence), and fear of the Lord (awe and wonder in God's presence).

grace—God's gift of friendship and a sharing in his life and love

Holy Spirit—the third Person of the Holy Trinity

Paraclete—advocate, consoler, or defender. Refers to Christ Jesus himself and the Holy Spirit whom he sent to guide and lead the Church to understand God's revelation to us through him.

CHAPTER SUMMARY

It is the Holy Spirit who binds us to Jesus Christ, enabling us to recognize him as God's own Son—our brother, Savior, and Lord. In this chapter we learned that:

1. The Holy Spirit is God, the third Person of the Holy Trinity, equal in dignity to the Father and the Son. We worship and glorify him.

2. The Holy Spirit came in power on Pentecost Sunday, emboldening the apostles and the Church to proclaim that Jesus is Lord God and Savior of the world. The Holy Spirit is the Paraclete, our Advocate.

3. The Holy Spirit is present with us in many ways as our Helper and Guide. He is especially present with us in the inspired Sacred Scriptures, Sacred Tradition, the Magisterium of the Church, the celebration of the sacraments, and through various gifts and ministries given to the Church.

4. The Spirit justifies us, forgives our sins, adopts us into God's family, empowers us to love as other Christs, and makes Christ's Paschal mystery and its fruits present to us.

5. Images used by the writers of Sacred Scripture and the Church for the Holy Spirit include breath, wind, fire, tongues of fire, water, and the dove.

6. The Spirit always works together with the Father and the Son. The Spirit was present and at work at creation and has always been present and at work in the world, bringing about God's plan of love and goodness for us and all creation together with the Father and the Son.

7. The Holy Spirit was present throughout the ministry, life, preaching, miracle-working, passion, death, resurrection, and glorification of Jesus Christ. He shared a joint mission with the Son. Jesus is head of his Body, the Church. The Holy Spirit is the soul of the Church.

EXPLORING OUR CATHOLIC FAITH

1. Listening to God's Word

The Spirit of God speaks to us through Sacred Scripture. Read 1 Corinthians, chapters 12 and 13. What does this passage tell you about yourself as a member of the Body of Christ?

2. Understanding the Teachings of the Catholic Church

In the *Dogmatic Constitution on the Church* the Church teaches: "When the work which the Father gave the Son to do on earth (see John 17:4) was accomplished, the Holy Spirit was sent on the day of Pentecost in order that he might continually sanctify the Church, and that, consequently, those who believe might have access through Christ in one Spirit to the Father" (see Ephesians 2:18) [4]. What does it mean to say that the Spirit's work is to continually "sanctify the Church"?

3. Reflecting on Our Catholic Faith

Reflect on this statement of faith: "The Christian's heart is the Spirit's home." In what ways does this insight help you live as a follower of Christ? Write your reflection in your journal.

4. Living Our Catholic Faith

Quietly read and reflect on Galatians 5:16–26. List all the ways you see each of the fruits of the Spirit in your life.

CHAPTER 6

The Holy Trinity: One God in Three Persons

The grace of the Lord Jesus Christ and
the love of God and the fellowship of
the holy Spirit be with all of you.

2 CORINTHIANS 13:13

What Do You Think?

In the space provided, write whether you agree or disagree with this statement. Give reasons for your opinion.

The Church's belief in the Holy Trinity—there is one God in three Persons—is a strict mystery. This means we could never have known that God is Father, Son, and Holy Spirit unless God revealed this to us.

There is a famous legend about Saint Augustine (a church Father and one of history's greatest theologians). One day Augustine was walking on the beach, contemplating the great mystery of God. There, he met a young boy who was taking water from the sea with a small bucket and pouring it into a hole he had dug in the sand. Time and again the young boy went back to the ocean, filled his bucket, and dumped it into the hole.

Curious, Saint Augustine finally asked, "Why do you keep pouring water into that hole?"

The boy replied, "Isn't it plain to see? I'm putting the ocean into this hole."

Saint Augustine had to laugh. "That's impossible," he replied. "The great sea is way too large for that small hole."

With love in his eyes, the little boy looked up and simply said, "And God is too big for your little mind." Suddenly, the boy disappeared.

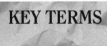

KEY TERMS

Holy Trinity

missions of the Holy Trinity

mystery

What images of God do you have? List them and discuss them with your group. What do they tell you about your understanding of the mystery of God?

This incident may or may not have happened to Saint Augustine. But the point of the story is well made: God is too big for the human mind to fully comprehend. This chapter will briefly explore our faith in the **Holy Trinity.**

(*Catechism of the Catholic Church,* 235, 237)

The Mystery of the Holy Trinity

In this chapter we will first look at what Jesus revealed about God: God is the Father, the Son, and the Holy Spirit. We will then examine church teachings about this foundational **mystery** of our faith. Finally, we will reflect on how God's loving goodness manifests itself in the two missions or works of the persons of the Holy Trinity—redemption and sanctification.

The Central Mystery of the Christian Faith

The mystery of the Holy Trinity is the most fundamental and essential teaching of the Christian faith. Our belief in the Holy Trinity is a "strict mystery." This means two things. First, it is something revealed to us by God about God that we could never have come to know had God not made it known to us. Second, we can never fully understand the meaning of this truth about God. As the young boy said to Augustine, "God is too big for your little mind."

We believe that Jesus Christ revealed this truth about God's identity to us.

Symbol for the Trinity

Triquetra

The triquetra is a design consisting of three equal arcs that emphasize equality among the three Persons of the Blessed Trinity. The interwoven arcs have no apparent beginning or end, signifying the eternal nature of each Person in the Blessed Trinity. The interlacing also represents unity among God as Father, Son, and Holy Spirit. The center of the triquetra forms a triangle, another ancient symbol of the Blessed Trinity.

Because of our faith in Jesus Christ and our trust in his Body, the Church, we believe there is one God who is Father, Son, and Holy Spirit—a Holy Trinity.

The Heart of Jesus' Revelation of God's Identity

The first Christians who met Jesus came to believe that Jesus was equal to God, that Jesus was indeed the Son of God dwelling among us. We share that faith, which has been passed on to us by the apostles.

The first Christians also came to believe that this same God was present with them in the Spirit that the Lord promised would remain with them after his life on earth. This Advocate was poured out on the disciples on Pentecost Sunday (Acts 2:1–4). We believe this Spirit is with us today. Just as the apostles and first believers in Jesus shared their faith, we share our faith and welcome others into the Church in the name of God, who Jesus revealed to us. We say, "I baptize you in the name of the Father, and of the Son, and of the Holy Spirit."

We believe in the Holy Trinity because Jesus—the Way, the Truth, and the Life—teaches us who God really is. The Father loves us so much that he sent the Son and the Spirit to us. He invites us to share—in a mysterious way—the very life and love of the Triune God, both here on earth and after death in eternal life. This is the most wonderful thing that can possibly happen to us. It is the heart of the good news!

God in Our Life

Recall major events in your own personal life, in your family life, and in the life of your civic community. How did these events make known to you the presence of God as Father, Son, or Holy Spirit? Share your responses with others.

My Personal Life:

My Family Life:

My Community Life:

Journal Writing: What is the most powerful way that you have come to know God's presence with you?

(CCC, 232–258)

One God in Three Persons

Christians are baptized in the name of the Triune God: "in the name of the Father and of the Son and of the Holy Spirit." In the doxology, which concludes the Eucharistic Prayer, we also profess our faith in the Holy Trinity. We pray "through him, with him, in him, in the unity of the Holy Spirit, all honor and glory is yours, almighty Father, forever and ever."

God the Father

One of the many ways people approach God in prayer is as "Father." In a special way, God also revealed himself to the people of Israel as Father. They trusted and believed that God is Creator, Provider, and Protector.

God's Revelation
·········· Through Israel ·········

The writings of the Old Testament clearly attest to the Israelites' faith in God as Father. God created the world, fathered the Covenant with the Chosen People, gave them the Law, and served as their true King and Ruler. The people of Israel especially came to believe God to be the "Father of the Poor," who cared for and protected the defenseless. They prayed,

> "Father of the fatherless, defender of widows—
> this is the God whose abode is holy"
> (Psalm 68:6).

God's Revelation
········· Through Jesus ·········

Jesus, a devout Jew, clearly continued to reveal God as Father—but in an "unheard-of sense." Yes, God is the caring, loyal, faithful, and forgiving Father of his son, Israel (Exodus 4:22), whom the people of Israel came to know and trust.

But Jesus taught God is more: God is not only the Father, the almighty Creator; God is also the Father of a Son who is equally and truly God—the unique Son who shares God's own nature. Jesus encourages us to pray constantly to God "our Father," who always hears us and responds to us. Throughout his life on earth Jesus spoke of God as Father in such a unique way that it revealed to his followers he was truly the Son of God, one with and equal to God the Father. Jesus spoke of "my heavenly Father" (Matthew 15:13). He taught his followers,

"No one knows the Son except the Father" (Matthew 11:27).

Jesus expressed his own unity with the Father by calling him *Abba,* a simple term of endearment expressing love and trust. Marvelously, Jesus invited us to address God as Abba in our prayers. We mere creatures are privileged to use such an intimate term to address the very Creator of the Universe! What Jesus has revealed is that his Father has adopted us into the divine family.

Jesus' whole ministry reveals a loving, merciful Father. Through Jesus we come to know and believe in God the Father as incredibly loving and forgiving.

Jesus' healing miracles reveal a compassionate God. The parable of the prodigal son (Luke 15:11–32), for example, drives home this truth about God.

But most dramatically and clearly, in the Paschal mystery of Jesus, the

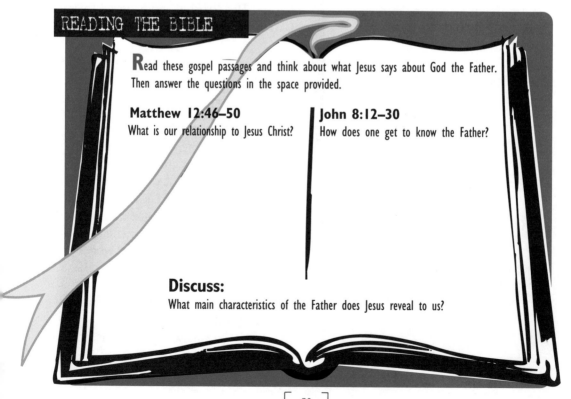

READING THE BIBLE

Read these gospel passages and think about what Jesus says about God the Father. Then answer the questions in the space provided.

Matthew 12:46–50
What is our relationship to Jesus Christ?

John 8:12–30
How does one get to know the Father?

Discuss:
What main characteristics of the Father does Jesus reveal to us?

Father is revealed as the One who gives us his own self-sacrificing Son for our salvation. Through this Son in the Holy Spirit, the Father redeems us. He raised his Son from the dead, and he will raise us through this very Son.

God the Son

By sending the Holy Spirit on Pentecost Sunday, the Father and the Son reveal the full mystery of the Blessed Trinity.

The apostles and the first church community believed Jesus to be the Word of God (John 1:1–5), "the image of the invisible God" (Colossians 1:15). The Gospels and other New Testament writings clearly witness to this faith in many ways. The early evangelists portrayed the beginning of Jesus' public ministry as the work of the Holy Trinity. Luke writes:

> After all the people had been baptized and Jesus also had been baptized and was praying, heaven was opened and the holy Spirit descended upon him in bodily form like a dove. And a voice came from heaven, "You are my beloved Son; with you I am well pleased." **Luke 3:21–22**

The many miracles also attest to God working through Jesus in curing lepers, the deaf, blind, and lame; driving out demons; mastering the forces of nature; and conquering death by raising the dead.

Likewise, the resurrection stories confirm the faith of early Christians in the divinity of Christ. Filled with the power of the Holy Spirit, the disciples proclaimed him Lord.

The early church councils of Nicaea (A.D. 325) and Constantinople (A.D. 381) summarized this faith: Jesus, the Son of God, is "consubstantial" with the Father, that is, having the same nature as God. He is God! We profess this same faith together in the Nicene Creed.

God the Holy Spirit

In chapter 5 we saw how the Lord promised to send the Paraclete to be with his disciples after he walks the way of suffering, death, and resurrection. After the Lord's ascension, his glorified body cannot be seen by us as it was to the disciples, who knew him during his earthly ministry. But the Lord has not abandoned us. He has

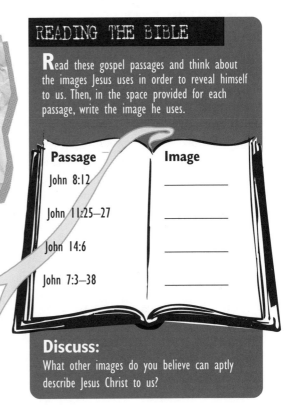

READING THE BIBLE

Read these gospel passages and think about the images Jesus uses in order to reveal himself to us. Then, in the space provided for each passage, write the image he uses.

Passage	Image
John 8:12	_____
John 11:25–27	_____
John 14:6	_____
John 7:3–38	_____

Discuss:
What other images do you believe can aptly describe Jesus Christ to us?

sent the Holy Spirit, who is the very presence of the risen, glorified Lord, the Spirit of love who always existed with the Father and the Son.

The Holy Spirit draws us to the Son and gives us the faith to proclaim him our Lord and Savior. This same Spirit empowers us to proclaim that God is our loving Father, the origin of all the good gifts the gracious Triune God showers on us.

The Sign of the Cross

**"In the name
of the Father
and of the Son
and of the Holy Spirit.
Amen."**

With this short blessing we sign ourselves, perhaps many times a day, we profess our faith in the Holy Trinity, one God in three Persons.

When we make the large sign of the cross with our right hand on our forehead, over our heart, and on our shoulders with outstretched hand, we are stating that we are completely under the power of the Redeemer. When we make the small sign of the cross with our thumb on our forehead, lips, and over our heart, we are asking God to bless our thoughts, words, and desires.

Throughout our lives, we profess our faith each and every day. We bless ourselves, using the sign of the cross. We profess our faith in the Holy Trinity. We remind ourselves who we are and who we have become—sharers in the life and love of God. The connection to our baptismal commitment is clear: We belong to the Holy Trinity.

The Inner Life of God

One God in three Persons? How can this be? Believers, guided by the Spirit, have struggled through the centuries to understand and to explain this profound mystery of our faith. In their efforts to do so, the great teachers of our faith distinguish between the inner life of God and the many works God has performed out of love for us to reveal and communicate his divine life.

From the beginning of the Church, formulas such as Paul's salutation to Christians living in the city of Corinth (2 Corinthians 13:13) have expressed the Church's belief in the Holy Trinity.

Later councils of the Church—the councils of Nicaea in A.D. 325 and Constantinople in A.D. 381—approved carefully worded statements that officially and authentically stated the Church's understanding of the Holy Trinity. In addition, the great teachers of the Church developed a vocabulary, or language, of faith to help express the mystery of the Holy Trinity.

Three key terms you will often see in reference to the Holy Trinity are *substance, nature,* and *essence.* These terms are used interchangeably to refer to the truth that God is one divine being. The term *person* refers to the truth that we believe there is a "distinction of relationship" between the Father, the Son, and the Holy Spirit.

.... Dogma of the Trinity ....

Given this vocabulary as background, this is what the Church teaches about God's own inner life.

❏ **The Trinity is one God.** There are not three Gods. The Father is wholly

God; the Son is wholly God; the Holy Spirit is wholly God. There are not three separate consciousnesses or intelligences or wills in one God. God is one—a unity-in-community.

❏ **The divine Persons are distinct.** The distinctions are from their relations. The Father generates, the Son is begotten by the Father, and the Holy Spirit proceeds from the Father and the Son. The Father is wholly in the Son and in the Holy Spirit; the Son is wholly in the Father and in the Holy Spirit; the Holy Spirit is wholly in the Father and in the Son.

·········· Analogies ··········

The great teachers of our faith often used analogies to help us understand this and other mysteries of our faith. An **analogy** is a comparison that helps us understand what it resembles, what it is similar to but not identical to. Saint Augustine (A.D. 354–430) used an analogy of thinking and loving to try to explain these relationships. From all eternity God the Father knew himself perfectly. This perfect knowledge is his Word, the Son, whom he generates from all eternity. The Son, or second Person of the Trinity, is the Father's perfect, divine expression of himself. The Father and the Son are totally one, yet distinct.

The relationship between the Father and the Son is a perfect relationship of love that is eternal and divine. This perfect love proceeds from both Father and Son, binding them into a community of unity. This love is the third Person of the Trinity, the Holy Spirit. The Holy Spirit is the perfect expression of love between the Father and the Son.

My Understanding of the Mystery of the Holy Trinity

Saint Augustine's and Saint John Damascene's analogies give us an insight into the meaning of realities that are difficult for us to understand. We should never confuse them with the profound mystery that helps us understand. Think of an analogy that helps you gain some insight into the mystery of the Holy Trinity. Write it here.

Saint John Damascene (A.D. 645?–750?) used two other analogies. First, he used the analogy of a tree: the Father is the root, the Son is the branches, and the Spirit is the fruit. The substance of each (root, branch, and fruit) is all the same—that of a tree—yet there is distinction. It is similar with the Holy Trinity. Each Person has the fullness of the divine nature; yet, there is distinction—one God, three Persons. Second, he used the image of the sun. The Father is the sun, the Son is the rays, and the Holy Spirit is heat. All are distinct, but all are within the same substance.

(CCC, 257–260)

The Work, or Missions, of the Holy Trinity

We also learn about the Holy Trinity by reflecting on God's works throughout salvation history. Reflecting on the ways we have come to know that God has revealed himself throughout salvation history and manifested himself to us throughout our own personal history helps us see there is one God, who is Father, Son, and Holy Spirit.

As we saw above, each of the divine Persons, though distinct, works as one. All are involved in the common work of salvation. However, each Person of the Trinity performs this common work according to his unique personal properties, or attributes. This is why we attribute the work of creation to God the Father Almighty, which he continues to keep in existence. We attribute the work of salvation to the Son, who lived in our midst, teaching and revealing the Father's love. We attribute the work of sanctification to the Holy Spirit, who is the love of God dwelling in each of us.

What the Documents Say

By calling God "Father," the language of faith indicates two main things: that God is the first origin of everything and transcendent authority; and that he is at the same time goodness and loving care for all his children. God's parental tenderness can also be expressed by the image of motherhood (see Isaiah 66:13; Psalm 131:2), which emphasizes God's immanence, the intimacy between Creator and creature. The language of faith thus draws on the human experience of parents, who are in a way the first representatives of God for man. But this experience also tells us that human parents are fallible and can disfigure the face of fatherhood and motherhood. We ought therefore to recall that God transcends the human distinction between the sexes. He is neither man nor woman: he is God. He also transcends human fatherhood and motherhood, although he is their origin and standard (see Psalm 27:10; Ephesians 3:14; Isaiah 49:15): no one is father as God is Father.

Catechism of the Catholic Church, 239

Creation

God makes himself known through creation—its beauty and majesty, its complexity and wonder. God has revealed himself to be the **Father,** the Creator. Jesus further revealed this Creator is not fearsome, distant, or uncaring, but Abba—Father—rich in mercy, love, and compassion.

Incarnation of the Son of God

God has already revealed himself through the incarnation of the **Son** of God—God-made-flesh—Jesus Christ. He is "Emmanuel," God-with-us. He is "Savior," God-for-us. In the incarnate Son of God, we have experienced God with a human face. In Jesus we have met a Lord and Savior who deeply cares for us.

Gifts of the Holy Spirit

God has revealed himself as the Holy Spirit, as an abiding presence dwelling within us. We have come to know the Holy Spirit as the giver of life and dispenser of gifts. This Holy Spirit is God living within us. Closer to us than we are to ourselves, the Holy Spirit guides, comforts, strengthens, and prays in us; the Holy Spirit unites us to Christ Jesus, who takes us to the Father.

The Church calls these the **missions of the Holy Trinity:** the sending of the Son for our redemption, and the sending of the Holy Spirit for our sanctification. However, all three Persons act as one and are fully present in all the missions.

We were made out of love and for love. The goal of our life is union with God—Father, Son, and Holy Spirit—each Person of the Trinity, without ever separating them.

We image God when we know, love, and serve him; we do this by joining others in community. We live our life with God when we approach him with others and reach out in love to our brothers and sisters. When we love others, we image the Triune God who is love, who lives among us.

One great sign of Christian life is simply this: We go to God together. As we will see in the next chapter, the Church, the Body of Christ and Temple of the Holy Spirit, is the wonderful means the Lord Jesus left us. As a community we draw close to the Triune God and to each other. We continue the work of the Lord, the work of the Trinity, here on earth.

Prayer

God be in my head,

and

in my understanding.

God be in my eyes,

and

in my looking.

God be in my mouth,

and

in my speaking.

God be in my heart,

and

in my thinking.

God be at my end,

and

at my departing.

REVIEW

IMPORTANT TERMS TO KNOW

analogy—a comparison that helps us partially understand what it resembles, what it is similar to but not identical to

Holy Trinity—our belief that there is one God in three Persons—the Father, the Son, and the Holy Spirit. Our belief in the Holy Trinity is the central belief of our Christian faith.

missions of the Holy Trinity—the special works in salvation history attributed to the second and third Persons of the Trinity: the Son, who alone became incarnate is the savior, and the holy Spirit, who alone descended is the sanctifier. While we attribute specific works to each person of the Trinity, each work is the common work of the three divine Persons who possess one and the same nature.

mystery—a term that means "hidden"; used by the writers of the Sacred Scriptures to name God's loving plan of love and forgiveness

CHAPTER SUMMARY

Belief in the Holy Trinity is the central belief of the Christian community. In this chapter we learned that:

1. Jesus revealed to us that there is one God who is Father, Son, and Holy Spirit. This is a strict mystery of faith. We know and believe it because God freely revealed it. Our minds can never fully understand it.

2. God not only shares knowledge about his inner life with us but also invites us to share in his very life and love, both in this life and forever in an eternal life of happiness.

3. Reflecting on God's works, the divine "economy," sheds light on who God is.

4. We believe there is one God in three Persons. God is one divine being. There are three distinct Persons in one God. They are God the Father, God the Son, and God the Holy Spirit. The Father generates the Son from all eternity. The Son is always begotten by the Father. The Holy Spirit proceeds as the love between the Father and the Son.

5. The divine economy (work) of the Holy Trinity refers to God's loving work for us. We attribute creation to the Father, redemption (salvation) to the Son, and sanctification to the Holy Spirit. However, because God is one, the three divine Persons are all involved in the common work of God among us.

EXPLORING OUR CATHOLIC FAITH

1. Listening to God's Word

Read and think about chapter 14 and chapter 15 of the Gospel according to John. What do we come to know about God from reading these two chapters? What do we come to know about ourselves?

2. Understanding the Teachings of the Catholic Church

Through the prayers of our Church we profess and celebrate our faith. Each and every eucharistic prayer concludes by the Church saying or singing: "Through him, with him, in him, in the unity of the Holy Spirit, all glory and honor is yours, almighty Father, forever and ever. Amen." What are we professing when we join in singing or saying this acclamation?

3. Reflecting on Our Catholic Faith

Saint John Eudes (1601–1680) shares this insight about prayer with us: "If you contemplate God with the eyes of faith, you will see him just as he is, in a certain manner, face to face." Place yourself in God's presence. Look at him face-to-face. Write your thoughts in your journal.

4. Living Our Catholic Faith

The missions or work of the Trinity refer to God's plan of loving goodness and salvation for us. We share in this work. List ways you can work with others to announce and make real God's plan of loving goodness that has come about in your family or in your community.

CHAPTER 7

The Church, the People of God

"I am the vine, you are the branches. Whoever remains in me and I in him will bear much fruit, because without me you can do nothing."

JOHN 15:5

Take the time to recall the many things that you have already learned about the Church. Use these incomplete statements as a guide.

1. The founder of the Church is . . .

2. The four marks of the Church are . . .

3. The Church is a sacrament because . . .

4. Some of the images to help us understand the true nature of the Church are the People of God and . . .

5. The Church has the charism to teach infallibly on . . .

What questions about the Church do you have?

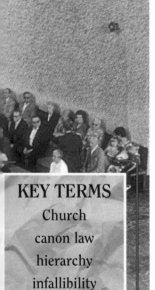

A stranger came to the parish church one Sunday morning and took a prominent seat at the front of the church. Everyone's eyes were glued on him because he wore a baseball cap on his head. Shortly before the celebrant processed to the altar, an usher gingerly approached the visitor and asked, "Do you know that you forgot to remove your hat?"

"Yes," said the man. "I left it on for a reason. You see, I'm new in this parish and have been coming to Mass here for the last two months. Yet no one has ever welcomed me. I figured this was a good way to get attention and, perhaps, someone might talk to me. Thank you! I'll be happy to remove my hat."

KEY TERMS

Church

canon law

hierarchy

infallibility

laity

mystery

sacrament

What are some ways your parish welcomes new members? In what ways can you make others feel a welcome part of your parish community?

How sad this newcomer felt so unwelcome and unnoticed in his new parish. Jesus was known for his hospitality, for welcoming people, for making them feel at home. Minimally, we should make everyone feel welcome in our churches. In this chapter we will be looking at the Church, a one-of-a-kind community formed and sustained by the Holy Spirit.

(*Catechism of the Catholic Church*, 748–780)

The Holy Catholic Church

Catholics are called the People of God, the family of believers in Jesus Christ. Today, we use the word **church** to refer to three interrelated realities: (1) the Christians who assemble to worship, (2) the local parish community, and (3) the universal community of believers.

This Church is a unique community that the Holy Spirit calls and forms to be other Christs. The Lord loves us as individuals and as his people. By the power of the Spirit, he unites us into a family for us to experience and to grow strong in his love. In doing so, we might take his good news out to others who so desperately need to hear it. Translated from the Greek *ekklesia,* the term *church* means "assembly," "convocation," "those called out." The Israelites used the term to refer to themselves as God's Chosen People. Christians use it to proclaim that they belong to the Lord Jesus Christ. In fact, the English word *church* comes from the word *kirche,* which means "what belongs to the Lord."

What we believe about this special assembly is intimately related to our belief in Jesus and the Holy Spirit. First, the Church is the vehicle the Lord Jesus uses to let his light shine into the world. Second, the Holy Spirit takes up his abode in the Church, calling it to holiness and endowing it with other attributes that the Nicene Creed terms the "marks" of the Church: one, holy, catholic, and apostolic.

The Church as a Mystery of God's Love

The Church is a mystery of God's love. It is both the means and goal of God's plan. Let us briefly investigate the term **mystery,** a religious term with rich overtones. The New Testament uses the term to describe "God's loving plan of goodness and forgiveness." Saint Augustine defined **sacrament** as a visible sign of an invisible grace. Pope Paul VI had a similar definition in mind when he called the Church "a reality imbued with the hidden presence of God."

When we call the Church a mystery, we are professing that the Church is both visible and spiritual, both a hierarchical society and the Mystical Body of Christ. The invisible God is working through this faith community, using it to continue Jesus' work of salvation. It is a hierarchically struc-tured society that is simultaneously Christ's mystical body, a visible society that is also a spiritual communion, an earthly community endowed with heavenly riches.

The Church as Sacrament of Salvation

The Church is the sacrament of the Holy Trinity's communion with humankind. It is the sign and instrument of communion between God and people. It is both the means and the goal of God's divine plan. Interestingly, the Latin word *sacramentum* translates the Greek word for mystery, *mysterion*. The bishops at the Second Vatican Council taught:

> By her relationship with Christ, the Church is a kind of sacrament or sign of intimate union with God, and of the unity of all mankind. She is also an instrument for the achievement of such union and unity.
>
> *Dogmatic Constitution on the Church,* 1

This concept of sacrament also applies to the Church. It, too, is a special sign that actually contains and communicates the invisible, divine reality it signifies.

The Church is a concrete sign of Christ's presence to all people. But, by the power of the Holy Spirit who resides in the Church, it is an instrument in the hands of the Lord. He uses his Church to touch all humans with his saving love, calling them into union with himself and each other.

Jesus the Lord is himself the first sacrament of God's love; he is the visible sign and image of God who takes us to the Father. Jesus uses his Church as a way to be present in our midst, though in a hidden way, to continue his work of salvation. An important way to describe this reality is the image of Church as our Lord's Mystical Body.

SYMBOL OF THE CHURCH

The Vine and the Branches

The Church is Christ's vineyard. Christ is the vine; we are the branches. This image or symbol for the Church helps us understand the "union" that exists between Christ and his followers. If we as individuals and as a Church stay united to Christ, we will bear much fruit. Cut off from Christ, we are dead. (See John 15:5.)

Your Own Image: In the space provided, draw your own image of the Church that helps express the "communion" that exists between Christ and the Church, between God and people. Explain its meaning.

The Church in God's Plan

We believe that each Person of the Holy Trinity had a role in the planning of the Church and its coming into historical reality. The Church was foreshadowed from the beginning of creation when the Father made the world so all people would live in union with the loving Trinity. Further, the Church was first prepared for in the Old Covenant when God called Abraham so that Israel could be the sign of the future convocation of all nations.

In the fullness of time, Jesus Christ instituted the Church out of his Paschal mystery of self-sacrifice—the mystery of love we celebrate in the Eucharist. Christ's reign is already mysteriously present in this community to which he taught a new way of acting and a prayer of its own.

The Lord sent the Holy Spirit to the Church to sanctify, guide, and direct it on its mission of preaching to all nations and making them disciples. And the Spirit showers his gifts on members of the Church to help them fulfill its Christ-appointed mission.

(CCC, 781–801)

Images of the Church

Because the Church is a mystery, a communion of the divine and the human, the visible and the spiritual, many images are used to help us understand it. Three of the most important images are the People of God, the Body of Christ, and the Temple of the Holy Spirit. These three images help us understand that the Church is the sacrament of the Holy Trinity's communion with us.

The People of God

The image of the Church as the People of God has its roots in the Old Testament covenant where God wished to sanctify and save not only individuals, but individuals who were also part of a loving community. Salvation history records how God taught, preserved, and loved the Israelites. His loving care for them prepared for the new People of God formed in the covenant of Jesus' sacrifice. The New Covenant, sealed in the Lord's blood, invites all people everywhere to unity in the Holy Spirit.

We believe that a person enters the People of God by faith and baptism. The image of the People of God clearly expresses our faith that we belong to God, having been born anew by faith and baptism in the Holy Spirit. Jesus the Christ is our head. His Spirit anoints us to live the law of love as other Christs, to be salt and light. He guides us to the kingdom of God, begun already by God on earth, which we must help spread until its final perfection at the end of time.

Because the Church is God's people joined to Christ Jesus, all members share in the Lord's priestly, prophetic, and kingly ministries. These ministries enable God's people to be true missionaries. The word *missionary* means "one sent." We derive our mission from the Lord. And the Holy Spirit, whom the Lord has sent to be our Helper, is the "principal agent of the whole Church's

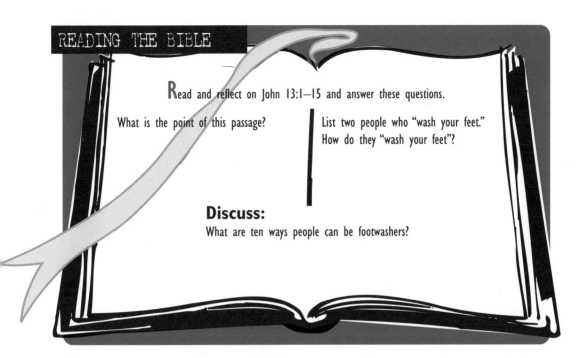

Read and reflect on John 13:1–15 and answer these questions.

What is the point of this passage?

List two people who "wash your feet." How do they "wash your feet"?

Discuss:

What are ten ways people can be footwashers?

mission." With the gifts of the Holy Spirit, the Lord sends us into the world to share his love so all people can be saved and know his truth. "As the Father has sent me, so I send you" (John 20:21).

There are four aspects to this mission:

❑ **Message.** God's people have the task of announcing the good news of salvation in Jesus Christ.

❑ **Community.** Saint John wrote: "This is how all will know that you are my disciples, if you have love for one another" (John 13:35). To be an effective sign of the Gospel, we must be a community who actually lives by faith, hope, and love. Christian fellowship will attract others to the Gospel.

❑ **Service.** By definition, a Christian is a person who serves others, especially the poor, lonely, imprisoned, sick, and suffering. The People of God must wash feet in imitation of the Lord and Master who showed the way at the Last Supper and by his sacrifice on Calvary.

❑ **Worship.** We humbly acknowledge that God is the source of our very being and all our gifts. We are a people whose words and lives give praise, adoration, and gratitude to God.

The Body of Christ

Jesus himself gave us the image of the Body of Christ. He taught that what we do for the least of our brothers and sisters we do to him (Matthew 25:40). Saint Paul also considered the Body of Christ a vital image of the Church. Paul realized the unity between Christ and his followers when the Lord appeared to him on his way to persecute Christians in Damascus. By persecuting his followers, the Lord told Saul (later Paul) that he was persecuting him (see Acts 9:4–5).

We believe that Christ lives in us and we live in him. By the power of the Holy Spirit, Jesus is one with his disciples, a unity mystically brought about in a special way in the Eucharist.

Nourished with the Body and Blood of Christ, we become the Body of Christ. Through this sacrament of love and unity, Paul later wrote to the Corinthians: "Now you are Christ's body, and individually parts of it" (1 Corinthians 12:27).

Union with the Lord as a member of his Body has several important implications:

❏ The risen, glorified Lord is present in the world today through us, his followers. We are the Lord's loving touch for the poor and persecuted. We are his compassionate glance and his comforting word. We are his instrument to preach the good news of God's salvation, the forgiveness of sins, and eternal life.

❏ Baptism incorporates us into Christ's Body. He is the head. We are the members. The Holy Spirit is the principle of union who makes us one body. The Spirit is the soul of the Church who overcomes natural divisions like color, race, nationality, and sex. He unites us into a family of brothers and sisters, God's family.

❏ Each member, no matter how seemingly insignificant, has tremendous dignity! In the unity of Christ's Body, there are different members and functions, but all work together for the common good. Just as each part of the human body has a specific and important purpose, so each member of the Church has a key role to play in building up the Body. The Spirit dispenses different gifts to each of us to accomplish our different functions. However, he gives each of us the greatest gift of all—the gift of love.

❏ Jesus, the head of his Body, the Church, unites each of us to his Passover. He gives us whatever gifts

we need to grow more like him. Christ Jesus and his Church, his Body, make up the whole Christ. The Church and Christ are one.

❏ Though we are one with Jesus the Lord, there is a clear distinction between Christ and his disciples. The image of the Church as the Bride of Christ underscores this difference. Bride and groom united in a conjugal union are one yet distinct. It is Jesus Christ who is the Bridegroom; he sacrificed for his bride (the Church). His sacrifice on the cross purified the Church and made her the mother of God's children.

What the Documents Say

The Church Is the Body of Christ

In the human nature united to himself, the son of God, by overcoming death through his own death and resurrection, redeemed man and changed him into a new creation (see Gal. 6:15; 2 Cor. 5:17). For by communicating his Spirit, Christ mystically constitutes as his body those brothers of his who are called together from every nation.

In that body the life of Christ is communicated to those who believe and who, through the sacraments, are united in a hidden and real way to Christ in his passion and glorification.

Dogmatic Constitution on the Church, 7

Discuss: Saint Paul used the image of a body and the interrelation of its parts to help us gain insight into the Church. In what ways does this image help you understand what it means to be a member of the Church? What other image might you use to express what it means to be a member of the Church?

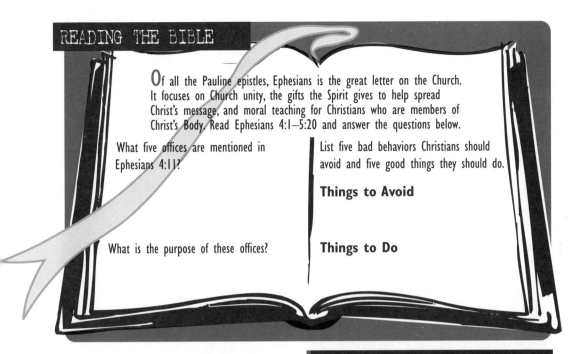

Of all the Pauline epistles, Ephesians is the great letter on the Church. It focuses on Church unity, the gifts the Spirit gives to help spread Christ's message, and moral teaching for Christians who are members of Christ's Body. Read Ephesians 4:1–5:20 and answer the questions below.

What five offices are mentioned in Ephesians 4:11?

List five bad behaviors Christians should avoid and five good things they should do.

Things to Avoid

What is the purpose of these offices?

Things to Do

The Temple of the Holy Spirit

Saint Augustine taught, "What the soul is to the human body, the Holy Spirit is to the Body of Christ, which is the Church" (CCC, 797; see *Sermon, 267,* 4: J. P. Migne, ed. *Patrologia Latina* [Paris: 1841–1855]). Our spirit penetrates every fiber of our body. Similarly, the Holy Spirit is ever-present in the Church: in the head who is Christ, in the whole body which is the Church, and in each member. He gives life to, unifies, makes holy, and builds up Christ's Body.

Because of the Spirit's all-pervasive presence in the Church, we can rightly call the Church the Temple of the Holy Spirit. This Temple is, in the words of the *Catechism of the Catholic Church*, "the sacrament of the Holy Trinity's communion" with us (747). The unity in the Church flows from the unity of the Triune God.

The Holy Spirit uses the Church to bring about God's saving works. He uses the Scriptures, the sacraments, graces, virtues, and special gifts given to individuals. These gifts or charisms are under the direction of church leaders and are to be used for the common good.

(CCC, 871–933)

Christs Faithful

A member of the Catholic Church is baptized, accepts the Lordship of Jesus, and works for God's kingdom. Baptism confers on each Christian equal dignity and a share in Christ's priestly (sanctifying), prophetic (teaching), and kingly (governing) offices. These three offices correspond to three basic ministries, or ways to serve God, in the Church.

Jesus established the hierarchy (pope and bishops) on the apostles and their successors. The hierarchy holds the Christ-appointed offices of teaching, sanctifying, and governing the Christian community. Helped by priests, their co-workers, and by deacons, the bishops have the duty of authentically teaching the faith, celebrating divine worship, and guiding their Churches as true pastors.

The laity are all those not in holy orders or members of a Church-approved religious state. They are called to be witnesses to Christ in all circumstances and are at the very heart of the human community. They are to serve as leaven in the world.

Those in consecrated life could be members of the hierarchy or the laity. They commit themselves to the vows of poverty, chastity, and obedience by living a special life dedicated to God that is recognized by the Church. Rooted in Baptism and dedicated totally to God, the religious state is "one way of experienceing a 'more intimate consecration'" to God (CCC, 916).

Consecrated life includes hermits, consecrated virgins, secular institutes, various apostolic societies, and those in religious orders like the Franciscans and Dominicans. "Religious life" is marked by its liturgical character; public profession of the vows of poverty, chastity (celibacy), and obedience; life in common; and a unique witness to the Lord's union with his Church. Their witness is a gift to the Church and a special sign to the world of the mystery of redemption.

The Prophetic Ministry

A prophet speaks for God. All the faithful share in the prophetic or teaching mission of Christ. For example, qualified laypeople can serve as catechists. Christian parents serve as evangelists who share the Lord's good news with their children. Baptism requires each Christian to witness, in word and deed, to the Lord's truth.

"Just so, your light must shine before others, that they may see your good deeds and glorify your heavenly Father" (Matthew 5:16).

Jesus gave his Church the mandate to proclaim authentically and truthfully his word as it appears in Scripture and Tradition. The Holy Spirit has led the Church in truth through the centuries. And when he founded the Church, the Lord himself promised to remain with it in a special way, giving it its authority, mission, orientation, and goal. He is the source of ministry in the Church.

To help the Church carry on its mission through the ages, the Lord founded the Church along hierarchical lines. The hierarchy is the ordered grade of ordained leaders in the Catholic Church, a sacred leadership headed by the pope and the bishops and their assistants, priests, and deacons. Catholics believe that Jesus chooses to teach, to rule, and to sanctify his Church through these ordained men. Theirs is a ministry of service; they preach the Gospel in Jesus' name and get their authority from him alone.

Today, the role of the hierarchy is to continue the ministry of Peter and the apostles. The Lord appointed them to continue his work on earth, to preserve the authentic tradition by ensuring that the true Gospel would be preached.

Peter's successor, the pope, is in the center and at the head of the bishops who succeed the apostles. He has Christ-given primacy over the whole Church. He enjoys by divine institution "supreme, full, immediate, and universal care of souls. He is the Vicar of Christ, and Pastor of the Universal Church. We base this belief on Christ's own teaching:

"And so I say to you, you are Peter, and upon this rock I will build my church."

Matthew 16:18

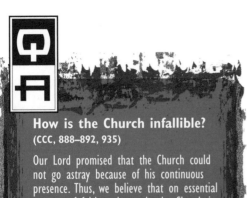

How is the Church infallible?
(CCC, 888–892, 935)

Our Lord promised that the Church could not go astray because of his continuous presence. Thus, we believe that on essential matters of faith and morals, the Church is infallible. Infallibility means that a certain doctrine is free from error. As the supreme pastor and teacher of the Church, the pope enjoys the gift of infallibility when he confirms his brethren in the faith by proclaiming as a definitive act, that is, intending to use his full authority in an unchangeable decision, defining a doctrine on faith or morals.

In union with the pope, the bishops as a group can also exercise this Christ-given gift of infallibility. They do so when they teach or protect Christ's revelation concerning belief or morality, for example, with the pope in an ecumenical council. The bishops can also exercise this Christ-given gift of infallibility when they teach collectively throughout the world in union with the pope.

When the Magisterium of the Church proposes a doctrine to be infallible, that is, as divinely revealed, Catholics owe it assent, the obedience of faith. This is so because such a teaching is backed by our Lord's own promise to remain with his Church through the Holy Spirit. If a person refuses to assent to such a teaching, he or she is guilty of heresy.

The Holy Spirit also helps the pope and bishops in their "ordinary teaching," which appears in encyclicals, pastoral letters, sermons, and the like. These teachings help us better understand divine revelation in matters of faith and morals. They also promote Christian love and service, and help in the proper administration of the sacraments and other spiritual and temporal benefits of the Church. As faithful Catholics, we must prayerfully listen to and follow these ordinary teachings; that is, we must give them religious assent.

The pope and the bishops form the college of bishops. The body of bishops has no authority unless it is united with the pope, Peter's successor and head of the college. In union with each other and Holy Father, the bishops are responsible for truthful teaching of God's Word. They do so in a special way in an ecumenical (worldwide) council. The pope is the bishop of Rome, the successor of Peter. He has a special role to be a living sign of unity in Christ for the universal Church, both for the bishops and all God's people. He speaks with the bishops as the voice of Jesus Christ alive in the Church. The individual bishop is, in a similar way, a foundation and visible source of unity in his own particular Church.

The Priestly Ministry

A major goal of the Church is the sanctification of people. Jesus himself came to make us holy, to bring us into union with his Father in friendship, to bestow on us a life of love and grace. Jesus formed a priestly people to bring everyone into contact with his Paschal mystery of love, the source of sanctification for all people. By definition, a priest serves as a go-between, a mediator between God and people. All Christians share in the Lord's priesthood, helping to bring others to God.

But you are "a chosen race, a royal priesthood, a holy nation, a people of his own, so that you may announce the praises" of him who called you out of darkness into his wonderful light. **1 Peter 2:9**

Many activities in the Church lead to holiness. For example, the teaching and ruling offices lead God's people to Christ, his truth and holiness. But Jesus left many other means of sanctification with his disciples: the sacraments, prayer, and Christian service. The ordained ministers in the Church have special authority to act in the place of Christ at the eucharistic sacrifice and to forgive sin in his name. Christ calls them to serve their Christian brothers and sisters through example, prayer, and their special ministry of the word and sacrament. However, their special vocation is not meant for the sake of the individual's personal glory but for the good and sanctification of all.

It is true that the Lord calls some to holy orders. However, he calls all Christians to holiness. Our baptism requires us to dedicate to Christ Jesus our work, prayer, family life, recreation, hardships—indeed, all aspects of our life. By offering them to God in the Eucharist, we make all aspects of our life holy. In a special way, husbands and wives, united to Jesus in holy matrimony, are a sign and source of holiness to each other and their children.

Finally, the Church invites laypeople to share their gifts in various ecclesial ministries, for example, as lectors or special ministers of the Eucharist.

The Church is both visible and spiritual, a hierarchical society and the Mystical Body of Christ. She is one, yet formed of two components, human and divine. That is her mystery, which only faith can accept.

Catechism of the Catholic Church, 779

The Kingly, or Regal, Ministry

A kingly or regal role calls to mind authority. The source of all authority in the Church resides in Jesus. He taught that "All power in heaven and on earth has been given to me" (Matthew 28:18).

The Lord shares his authority to teach with the hierarchy. Similarly, he shares his authority to govern and direct—necessary features for any institution to survive.

The Church's ruling office exists simply for the growth of faith and holiness. Those who exercise it should do so with humility, love, compassion, and understanding. Church leaders look to the Good Shepherd for guidance on how to rule:

But Jesus summoned them and said, "You know that the rulers of the Gentiles lord it over them, and the great ones make their authority over them felt. But it shall not be so among you. Rather, whoever wishes to be great among you shall be your servant; whoever wishes to be first among you shall be your slave. Just so, the Son of Man did not come to be served but to serve and to give his life as a ransom for many."

Matthew 20:25–28

Thus, the sole purpose for Church law, or canon law, is to help us live as holy

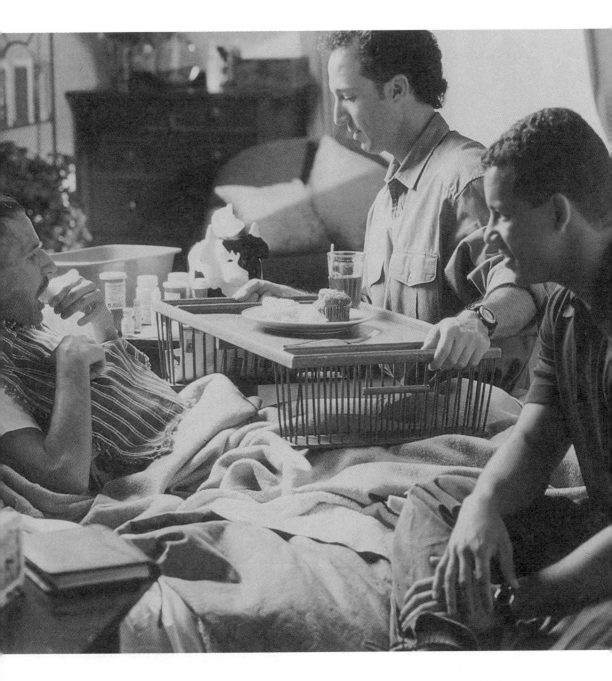

members of Christ's Body. Again, faithful Catholics owe Church law and the hierarchy's legitimate instructions respectful obedience; these regulations exist for the good of God's people.

The laity partake of the Lord's kingly ministry by striving to master sin in themselves and in the world through self-denial and by working for justice to promote the coming of God's kingdom on earth. Qualified laypeople may also be invited to serve on parish finance committees, councils, and other church organizations.

Prayer

Everyone in Christ's Body must help the Lord do his work, including the work of bringing peace to the world. A wonderful prayer in the Church's treasury is this famous Prayer for Peace, attributed to the great Saint Francis of Assisi. Commit it to memory and pray it often.

Lord, make me an instrument
   of your peace.
Where there is hatred, let me
   sow love;
where there is injury, pardon;
where there is doubt, faith;
where there is despair, hope;
where there is darkness, light;
where there is sadness, joy.
O Divine Master, grant that I
may not seek so much to be
consoled as to console;
to be understood,
   as to understand,
to be loved, as to love.
For it is in giving that we
   receive,
it is in pardoning that we are
   pardoned,
and it is in dying that we are
   born to eternal life.

REVIEW

IMPORTANT TERMS TO KNOW

Church—the community of Christian disciples who accept the one, holy, Catholic, and apostolic faith

canon law—the official body of Church laws that govern the life of the Catholic community

hierarchy—the official, sacred leadership in the Church. It includes the Church's ordained ministers—bishops, priests, and deacons. The pope, the bishop of Rome, is Saint Peter's successor. He is the Christ-appointed symbol of Church unity and authority.

infallibility—the Christ-given gift whereby the pope, and bishops teaching with him (for example, in an ecumenical council), are protected from error when proclaiming a doctrine related to Christian faith or morals

laity—all the members of God's people except the clergy (those ordained) and those in religious life

mystery—a reality filled with God's invisible presence. We often apply this term to God's plan of salvation in Jesus Christ, the Church, and the sacraments.

sacrament—an outward or visible sign of an invisible grace; a symbol that both points to a spiritual reality and brings it about. We apply this term to Christ Jesus, the great sign of God's love for us; to the Church, the continuing presence of the Lord in our midst; and to the seven sacraments—Baptism, Confirmation, Eucharist, Reconciliation, Anointing of the Sick, Matrimony, and Holy Orders.

CHAPTER SUMMARY

A Catholic, by definition, is a member of Christ's Body, the Church. In this chapter we learned that:

1. Church means "convocation," or "assembly"—"those called out" or "belonging to the Lord." The Church is a mystery of God's love. It is the sacrament of the Holy Trinity's communion with us. It is both the means and the goal in God's plan of salvation.

2. The Church is a reality filled with the hidden presence of God. It has a spiritual dimension and a visible aspect; it is a hierarchical society and the Mystical Body of Christ.

3. Because the Church is a mystery of divine love with deep significance, Scripture gives us many images of the Church. Three main images are the People of God, the Body of Christ, and the Temple of the Holy Spirit.

4. People of God underscores the fact that we belong to God. A person enters the People of God by faith and baptism. All people are called to belong to the People of God.

5. The Church is the Body of Christ in which there is a diversity of members and functions. Christ is the head of this Body. All members of the Church—hierarchy, laity, and those in consecrated life—share in Christ's prophetic, priestly, and kingly ministries.

6. The Church is the Temple of the Holy Spirit. The Holy Spirit is the soul of the Body of Christ, giving it life and making it holy.

7. The Lord promised to remain in the Church, guarding it in the truth. He blessed the Church with the gift of infallibility, which safeguards Christian truth when the pope, and bishops united to him, teach in matters of faith and morals. Catholics owe obedience of faith to infallible teachings of the Magisterium, whether pronounced by specific acts of the pope or council on the one hand or the general teaching of the bishops disbursed throughout the world in union with the pope on the other.

EXPLORING OUR CATHOLIC FAITH

1. Listening to God's Word

The New Testament uses many images to describe members of the Church. Here are some: children of God, saints, soldiers, ambassadors, servants, stewards, and witnesses. Choose several of these images. What do they tell you about who you are and who you are called to be?

2. Understanding the Teachings of the Catholic Church

The *Catechism of the Catholic Church* teaches us: "The Church is both visible and spiritual, a hierarchical society and the Mystical Body of Christ. She is one, yet formed of two components, human and divine. That is her mystery" (779). Thinking about what you learned in this chapter, what does that teaching mean? Discuss your insights with others.

3. Reflecting on Our Catholic Faith

In the prayer of Saint Francis of Assisi we pray, "Lord, make me an instrument of your peace." In what ways does this prayer call you to be a true follower of Christ? Write your thoughts in your journal.

4. Living Our Catholic Faith

The prayer of Saint Francis also contains a list of specific actions of a peacemaker. Reread the prayer on page 90 and with a small group of friends think about what this prayer calls us to do. Choose two of the actions and do them with a small group.

CHAPTER 8

The Catholic Church: One, Holy, Catholic, and Apostolic

So then you are no longer strangers and
sojourners, but you are fellow citizens with the
holy ones and members of the household of God,
built upon the foundation of the apostles and
prophets, with Christ Jesus himself as the capstone.
Through him the whole structure is held together
and grows into a temple sacred in the Lord;
in him you also are being built together
into a dwelling place of God in the Spirit.

EPHESIANS 2:19–22

In the space provided, write "A" if you agree with the statement, "D" if disagree with it, and "N" if you have no opinion. Be ready to explain your choices.

_____ 1. Ecumenism tries to work for unity among Christian churches.

_____ 2. The true source of the unity of the Church is believing Christians.

_____ 3. We say the Church is holy because its members cannot sin.

_____ 4. The word *catholic* means "universal," and the Church is catholic because all the graces necessary for salvation can be found in the Church.

_____ 5. Only baptized Christians can be saved.

A little girl went to church every week with her parents. Their parish church had some beautiful stained-glass windows, one of which illustrated the four gospel writers: Saints Matthew, Mark, Luke, and John.

One Sunday, the homily was about becoming a saint. After Mass, the girl's mother asked her child, "What is a saint?"

"That's easy, Mommy," the girl replied. "A saint is a person the light shines through."

How right this wise little girl is! A saint is indeed a person through whom the light of Christ shines. One of the early names for the Church was "the saints." This designation reminds us that the Lord calls us both as individuals and as a community to let his light shine through us so others might be drawn to him.

Brainstorm words and phrases that come to mind when you hear the word *saint*. Which of these apply to people who are alive? Do people only become saints after they die? Explain.

KEY TERMS

apostles

catholic

Catholic Church

ecumenism

marks of the Church

schism

In the Nicene Creed we profess, "We believe in one holy catholic and apostolic Church." These are the four marks, or four essential features, of the Church and her mission. These four essential features of the Church help us recognize her essential nature. They serve as a beacon to nonbelievers, attracting them to Christ Jesus. In this chapter we will examine more closely the four marks of the Church.

(*Catechism of the Catholic Church*, 813–822)

The Church Is One

The unity of the Holy Trinity—one God in three Persons—is the basis of the Church's unity. The Church is one because of her founder, Jesus Christ, and because of her soul, the one who gives her life, the Holy Spirit. The Lord Jesus prayed:

> "[T]hey may all be one, as you, Father, are in me and I in you, that they also may be in us, that the world may believe that you sent me."
>
> **John 17:21**

Visible bonds of unity in the Church include:

❏ the profession of one faith, traceable to the apostles;

❏ the common celebration of worship, especially the sacraments; and

❏ the succession of bishops from apostolic times through Holy Orders.

The mark of unity does not mean a rigid uniformity. There is great diversity of traditions within the Church, a diversity of both people and gifts. There is much room for local and cultural expressions of the Catholic faith. An example of this diversity includes the celebration of the Eucharist in the language of the people.

The Catholic Church and Other Christian Churches

Unfortunately, almost from the beginning of the Church, the unity of the Church Christ founded has been wounded. Disruptions in unity were caused by **heresy** (the denial of essential truths), **apostasy** (the denial of the faith), and **schism** (a break in unity).

While the unity Christ intended for his Church has been broken, all who have been baptized in Jesus are Christian. Members of the Orthodox Church and the many Protestant churches remain our brothers and sisters in Christ Jesus.

We believe that the "fullness of the means of salvation" is found in the Catholic Church. The Second Vatican Council definitively taught that the Church of Christ entrusted to Peter and his successors "subsists in the Catholic Church," which is governed by the pope and the bishops in union with him. It was to Peter and his successors that Jesus gave all the blessings of the New Covenant to establish the Body of Christ on earth.

Though the Catholic Church has the "fullness" of the means of sanctification intended by Christ Jesus, many means of holiness can be found outside the Catholic Church. The Church teaches:

Moreover, some, even very many, of the most significant elements and endowments which together go to build up and give life to the Church itself, can exist outside the visible boundaries of the Catholic Church: the written Word of God; the life of grace; faith, hope, and charity, with the other interior gifts of the Holy Spirit, as well as visible elements.

Decree on Ecumenism, 3

Working for Unity

All Christians—Catholics and non-Catholics—must continually pray for and work for perfect unity in the Church. All Catholics—clergy and laity, individuals and the larger community—can be involved in the work of **ecumenism.** Ecumenism is that movement that works to restore and promote unity in Christ's Church. Pope John Paul II describes the purpose of ecumenism:

Ecumenism is directed precisely to making the partial communion existing between Christians grow toward full communion in both truth and charity.

That All May Be One, 14

We live at a time when the Church is both fostering and practicing unity. Christians are praying to the Holy Spirit to try to achieve a greater degree of oneness in Christ. The Spirit calls us to work for the unity Christ intends for his Church by living holy lives, by constantly renewing ourselves according to gospel values. In addition, we can:

Pray. Prayer is the soul of the ecumenical movement. We should pray to the Holy Spirit to guide our efforts for Christian unity. Catholics should not just pray alone. We should pray with our Christian brothers and sisters for the Lord to lead us into truth.

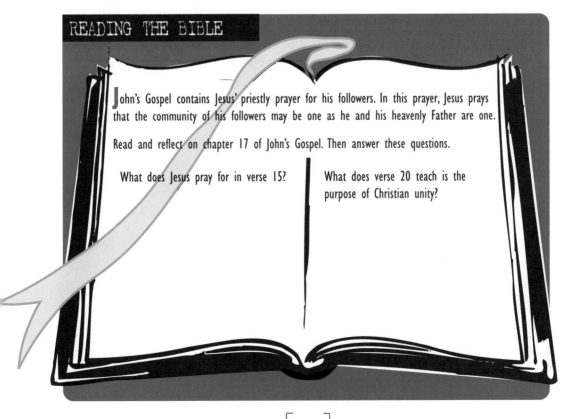

READING THE BIBLE

John's Gospel contains Jesus' priestly prayer for his followers. In this prayer, Jesus prays that the community of his followers may be one as he and his heavenly Father are one.

Read and reflect on chapter 17 of John's Gospel. Then answer these questions.

What does Jesus pray for in verse 15?

What does verse 20 teach is the purpose of Christian unity?

Study. We should strive to know and understand the teachings of our faith so that we can share it with others. We show respect when we learn about their religious communities. Mutual understanding can promote Christian unity.

Communicate. Catholics and other Christian scholars are continuously engaging in ecumenical dialogue. Individual Catholics should follow their example. Whenever we share our faith, Christian charity should always guide us as we express ourselves and listen to others express themselves.

Cooperate in service. Joining hands with other Christians in social action, service, and works of charity and justice can greatly promote Christian unity.

(CCC, 823–829)

The Church Is Holy

The second mark of the Church is holiness. The Church is the "holy people of God" (*Constitution on the Church*, 12). The members of the Church are called saints, or "holy ones." (See Acts 9:13; 1 Corinthians 6:1, 16:1.)

God—the Father, the Son, the Holy Spirit—is the ultimate source of all holiness. The Church is holy because we are the adopted children of the Father.

The Church is holy because we are the Body of Christ. Jesus, the Holy One, the Son of God, gave up his life to make the Church holy. The risen, all-holy Lord took the Church as his bride and dwells in it as its head.

The Church is holy because we are the Temple of the Holy Spirit. We profess that the Church is holy because the Holy Spirit lives in it. Jesus and the Father have sent the Holy Spirit to dwell with us, to sanctify the Church and make it one with the Holy Trinity, who alone is holy.

Our Call to Holiness

The Lord allows his life and light into the world through the Church, sanctifying it and each of its members. He has entrusted to the Church "the

What the Documents Say

The Church is holy: the Most Holy God is her author; Christ, her bridegroom, gave himself up to make her holy; the Spirit of holiness gives her life. Since she still includes sinners, she is "the sinless one made up of sinners." Her holiness shines in the saints; in Mary she is already all-holy.

Catechism of the Catholic Church, 867

When we describe the Church we say, "the Church is holy." At the same time, however, we say, "She includes sinners." How would you explain this paradox?

fullness of the means of salvation" and ways to achieve holiness—our life with God. Among these means of holiness in the Church are:

❏ the Word of God found in the Bible, Apostolic Tradition, the writings of great saints and theologians, and the teaching office of the Church;

❏ the liturgical life of the Church, including the sacraments, especially the Eucharist;

❏ the various prayer traditions practiced by the Church throughout the ages.

The best way to achieve holiness is to strive to love God above all else and to love our neighbor for the love of God. The early Christians quickly understood that it was not enough to simply profess faith in the Lord; our lives must also give witness to our faith. What we profess in word must be translated into deeds:

What good is it, my brothers, if someone says he has faith but does not have works? Can that faith save him? If a brother or sister has nothing to wear and has no food for the day, and one of you says to them, "Go in peace, keep warm, and eat well," but you do not give them the necessities of the body, what good is it? So also faith of itself, if it does not have works, is dead.

James 2:14–17

STRIVING FOR HOLINESS

Holiness involves living a Christian life, imitating the Lord. Paul, in Romans 12:9–16, gives a marvelous list of instructions on ways we can strive to live holy lives. Examine how well you are striving right now to be a holy, Christlike person. In the space provided, describe your response.

Let love be sincere; hate what is evil, hold on to what is good; love one another with mutual affection; anticipate one another in showing honor (Romans 12:9–10).

Do not grow slack in zeal, be fervent in spirit, serve the Lord (Romans 12:11).

Rejoice in hope, endure in affliction, persevere in prayer (Romans 12:12).

Contribute to the needs of the holy ones, exercise hospitality (Romans 12:13).

Bless those who persecute [you], bless and do not curse them (Romans 12:14).

Rejoice with those who rejoice, weep with those who weep (Romans 12:15).

Have the same regard for one another; do not be haughty but associate with the lowly; do not be wise in your own estimation (Romans 12:16).

People on the Way

Though the Church is holy, we, its members, are imperfectly holy—we are always on the road to deeper holiness. The Christian community is a paradox. The all-holy Christ Jesus meets us through people like us—people who are at the same time weak, lacking love, and sinful, yet courageous, always willing to give, and virtuous. Why? Because we are pilgrims—people on the way to meet God.

We call certain people holy because the light of Christ shines through their lives. Through the ages, despite the sins of individual Christians who obscure the Church's holiness, there have always been men and women whose lives have witnessed heroically to the Lord and his Gospel. The Church has canonized, or officially recognized, these people to be "saints," or "holy ones." The greatest of these saints is Mary, the Mother of God, and our Blessed Mother, too. "In her, the Church is already the 'all-holy'" (CCC, 829).

We often talk a good game but frequently fail to measure up. Holiness is "something" we are always working toward, with God's help and grace. We need constant conversion. We need to focus and refocus on God, who is always at the center of our lives. To grow in our relationship with God and one another, we must be humble. We need to strive for holiness. We need to admit our need for healing, for the forgiving touch of God, who welcomes us as his children.

(CCC, 830–856)

The Church Is Catholic

The third mark of the Church is catholicity. The second-century martyr-bishop Saint Ignatius of Antioch (died ca. 110) was the first to use the word **catholic** to describe the Church.

❏ The word *catholic* means "universal," or "general." The Church is catholic in two ways:

❏ The Church is catholic because Christ is present in his Church as its head. The Church, the Body of Christ, contains the fullness of the means of salvation: complete and correct confession of faith, the full life of the sacraments, and the ordained ministry that traces itself to the apostles.

❏ The Church is catholic because it has the command and responsibility to teach all nations as Christ commanded it to do. "Go, therefore, and make disciples of all nations, baptizing them in the name of the Father, and of the Son, and of the holy Spirit, teaching them to observe all that I have commanded you" (Matthew 28:19–20).

The Church Is Missionary

Being Christian involves proclaiming the good news to others. The members of the Church must continue to live up to the Lord's mandate to preach the Gospel to everyone. Just as the Father sends the Son and the Spirit to unite humanity with the Holy Trinity, Christ commissions his Church to continue to preach the message of salvation to all people in all places and at all times. This is why the Church is essentially missionary. We are missionaries, heralds of the Gospel, when we share the good news with nonbelievers, work unceasingly for Christian unity, and engage in a respectful dialogue with those who have not yet accepted the Gospel of the Lord. We accomplish this mission best when we proclaim the good news in a spirit of poverty and penance and imitate Jesus' own ministry of self-sacrificing service and love.

Membership in the Catholic Church

God invites everyone to share in his life and love. God invites everyone to salvation. And in God's loving plan of goodness, salvation comes through Jesus Christ and the Church, the Body of Christ in the world. Peter proclaimed this faith from the earliest days of the Church:

> "There is no salvation through anyone else, nor is there any other name under heaven given to the human race by which we are to be saved."
>
> **Acts 4:12**

Paul confirmed this teaching:

> For there is one God.
> There is also one mediator between God and the human race,
> Christ Jesus, himself human, who gave himself as ransom for all.   **1 Timothy 2:5–6**

Research two of these Christian churches: Baptist, Episcopalian, Lutheran, Methodist, Pentecostal, Presbyterian. Report on two beliefs or practices they have in common with Catholics and two beliefs or practices on which they disagree with Catholics.

Share your report with your group.

Christ calls everyone to belong to his Church. The Church must show and bring others to Jesus. As God's people, the Church is a sacrament of God's love—the way for the saving Christ to continue his work here on earth through the power of the Holy Spirit. As sincere people seek salvation, Christ's Church will attract them, and they will seek membership in his Body.

In different ways Catholics, other Christians, and all people whom God's grace calls to salvation either belong to or are "ordered" to this catholic unity.

[But those who are] fully incorporated into the Catholic Church are those who, possessing the Spirit of Christ, accept all the means of salvation given to the Church together with her entire organization, and who—by the bonds constituted by the profession of faith, the sacraments, ecclesiastical government, and communion—are joined in the visible structure of the Church of Christ, who rules her through the Supreme Pontiff and the bishops.
Dogmatic Constitution on the Church, 14

The Church and Non-Catholic Religions

There are many elements of holiness and truth outside the Catholic Church. Concerning these other religious groups, the Church teaches the following.

Non-Catholic Christians. Protestant and Orthodox churches believe in Jesus Christ and have been properly baptized. Those who believe in Christ and have been properly baptized are put in a certain although imperfect communion with the Catholic Church. Catholics acknowledge, respect, and praise what we have in common with the Protestant churches—faith in the Triune God; acceptance of the Bible; prayer; grace; the theological virtues of faith, hope, and love; the gifts of the Spirit; baptism; commitment to God's kingdom; and the desire to live a moral life.

Our communion with the Orthodox churches is profound. We share the basic beliefs and traditions up to the separation that occurred in the Great Schism of 1054. We accept the validity of all seven of their sacraments, including a legitimate hierarchy and priesthood. The major contending point is over the authority of the bishop of Rome, the pope.

Judaism. Jesus himself was a pious Jew. The Jewish faith is the spiritual parent of Christianity. Our Jewish cousins in the faith possess adoption by God, the Law and prophets, the first covenant as God's people, the worship of the one true God, God's promises, and the promise of the Messiah. All forms of anti-Semitism are loathsome and contrary to Jesus' message of love.

Islam. Muslims worship the one and merciful God. While they do not acknowledge the divinity of Jesus Christ, they honor him as a great prophet and recognize his mother, Mary. With Christians they profess the faith of Abraham, and look forward to a day of judgment and resurrection. They strive to live a moral life, and worship God through prayer, almsgiving, and fasting.

Other non-Christian religions. All people have been created out of love to know, love, and serve God. All people—regardless of religion—are essentially one human family, with a common origin and common destination. We recognize that all people of faith are on a quest for the one true God, who wills the salvation of all.

> [The Catholic Church] rejects nothing of what is true and holy in these religions. She has a high regard for the manner of life and conduct, the precepts and doctrines which, although differing in many ways from her own teaching, nevertheless often reflect a ray of that truth which enlightens all men.
>
> *Declaration on the Relationship of the Church to Non-Christian Religions, 2*

(CCC, 857–865)

The Church Is Apostolic

From the very beginning of his ministry, Jesus "appointed twelve [whom he also named apostles] that they might be with him and he might send them forth to preach" (Mark 3:14). The fourth mark of the Church is "apostolic." The term *apostolic* comes from the word *apostle*.

The term *apostle* means "emissary," or "one who is sent." This helps us understand the meaning of the fourth mark of the Church.

Christ founded the Church on the apostles and handed on to them the authority and responsibility to continue his work with the guidance of the Holy Spirit. They, in turn, passed this authority and responsibility on to their successors, whom we call bishops in union with the pope, who is the successor of Saint Peter.

Like Saint Peter and the first apostles whom Jesus chose and sent forth, the pope and the bishops have been chosen to continue to preach, govern, and sanctify the Church. With the help and guidance of the Holy Spirit promised by Christ (John 14:15–31), the Church continues to hand on the teaching of the apostles throughout the ages.

The Church is apostolic because the Church:

❏ is built on the foundation of the apostles;

❏ keeps and hands on the teaching she has heard from the apostles;

❏ continues to be taught, sanctified, and guided by the apostles through their successors.

All members of Christ's Body also have been called and sent forth to preach and live Christ's Gospel. The Spirit bestows gifts and talents on each and every member of the Church to build up and strengthen the Body of Christ to fulfill its mission, or apostolate, in the world (1 Corinthians 12:4–11).

The Catholic Church will always have the task to bring the Good News of Christ to all. Ours is the task to lead others to the Body of Christ, the Church, the community of God's people, the Temple of the Holy Spirit where humanity can discover its true unity and salvation. This is a task for the Church as a whole and for each member who is privileged to be a member of it.

We have the singular duty to proclaim the good news of Jesus to those who do not know it. In so doing, we help bring forth the truth and goodness that God has implanted in every human heart, leading all our brothers and sisters to eternal happiness in Christ Jesus.

A wise person observed, "The Church exists for a double purpose—gathering in and sending out." The Catholic Church assembles for Eucharist both to symbolize and to celebrate our unity in Christ. We do so to grow in holiness and unity with Christ and one another by receiving his Body and Blood in the Eucharist. We are also dismissed, or sent out, as apostles into the world to share the message and person of Jesus Christ to the countless millions who long desperately for his love and salvation.

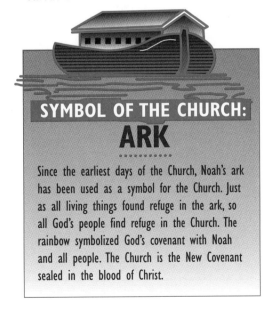

SYMBOL OF THE CHURCH:
ARK

Since the earliest days of the Church, Noah's ark has been used as a symbol for the Church. Just as all living things found refuge in the ark, so all God's people find refuge in the Church. The rainbow symbolized God's covenant with Noah and all people. The Church is the New Covenant sealed in the blood of Christ.

Prayer
of
Saint
Ignatius of Loyola

◇ ◇ ◇ ◇

Lord, teach me to be generous,

Teach me to serve you
as you deserve,

To give and not to count the cost,

To fight and not to heed the
wounds,

To toil and not to seek for rest,

To labor and not to ask for reward,

Save that of knowing
that I do your will.

Amen.

REVIEW

IMPORTANT TERMS TO KNOW

apostles—the "Twelve"; the leaders Jesus chose and sent forth to continue the work he began; the word *apostle* means "one who is sent," or "emissary." In its original sense, it referred to the Twelve whom Jesus chose to help him in his earthly ministry. The successors of the apostles are the bishops. In its broadest sense, the term refers to all of Christ's followers who must spread his message in word and deed.

catholic—a word derived from the Greek word meaning "universal," or "general." The Church founded by Christ is always open to all people everywhere and preaches the fullness of God's revelation in Jesus Christ.

Catholic Church—the People of God united in their acceptance of the pope and bishops as the successors of the apostles and in the celebration of the seven sacraments. The Catholic Church includes eight Catholic traditions of which the Roman Rite is the largest. The other seven traditions are Armenian, Byzantine, Chaldean (East Syrian), Coptic, Ethiopian, Maronite, and West Syrian.

ecumenism—the movement that seeks the union of all Christians and eventually the unity of all peoples throughout the world

marks of the Church—the four essential features of the Church and her mission. We profess that the Church is one, holy, catholic, and apostolic.

schism—a rupture in Christian unity that results from a group of Christians separating itself from the larger body of the Church

CHAPTER SUMMARY

1. We profess that the Church is one, holy, catholic, and apostolic. These four marks indicate the essential characteristics of the Church and her mission. The true Church of Jesus Christ "subsists in" the Catholic Church, governed by the pope and bishops in union with him.

2. God is the source of unity in the Church. The visible bonds of unity include the profession of one faith, common worship, and apostolic succession through the pope and bishops. In cooperation with the Holy Spirit, ecumenism works for unity among Christians. A spirit of repentance and self-renewal, prayer, study, communication, and shared service help foster Christian unity.

3. The Church is essentially holy because Jesus Christ and the Holy Spirit sanctify it. The Church is the Body of Christ and the Temple of the Holy Spirit. All the means of holiness necessary for salvation can be found in the Catholic Church.

4. The Church is catholic, or universal, because Jesus Christ, the Savior of all, is present in it and because the Church has been sent out on a mission to the whole world.

5. The Church is apostolic because it is built on the foundation of the apostles, hands on the teachings of the apostles, and continues to be taught, sanctified, and governed by the successors of the apostles with the help of the Holy Spirit who dwells in her.

6. The Church respects other religions. It acknowledges what is good, holy, and true in them.

EXPLORING OUR CATHOLIC FAITH

1. Listening to God's Word

Read and reflect on Matthew 28:16–20, Acts 1:8, and 1 Corinthians 15:7–8. What is the work and mission of the Church? What is your work and mission as a member of the Body of Christ, the Church?

2. Understanding the Teachings of the Catholic Church

Jesus prayed to his Father that his followers would be "one" as he and the Father are "one." Ecumenism works toward bringing about unity among Christians. Knowing about what unites us with and what separates us from other Christian churches is an important first step of the work of ecumenism. Research the beliefs and practices of these Christian churches. What two beliefs or practices do Catholics share with each? What two beliefs or practices do Catholics and each of these churches disagree on?

3. Reflecting on Our Catholic Faith

Saint Irenaeus, a second-century bishop and martyr, wrote, "Where the Church is, there is the Spirit of God; and where the Spirit of God is, there is the Church and all grace, and the spirit is truth." Reflect on the reality that you are a Temple of the Holy Spirit. Pray to the Spirit. Write your prayer in your journal.

4. Living Our Catholic Faith

At baptism, you were anointed with chrism with the words, "As Christ was anointed Priest, Prophet, and King, so may you live always as members of his body, sharing everlasting life. Amen" *(Rite of Baptism)*. Brainstorm ways you are challenged to live as a member of Christ's Body, the Church. How can others help you meet that challenge?

CHAPTER 9

Mary and the Communion of Saints

And Mary said:
   "My soul proclaims the greatness of the Lord;
     my spirit rejoices in God my savior.
   For he has looked upon his handmaid's lowliness;
     behold, from now on will all ages call me blessed."
                 LUKE 1:46–48

Write the correct choice in the space provided.

____ 1. The term *communion of saints* includes the idea that any good in one part of the Church's body can be communicated to others. (T or F)

____ 2. The Church includes: (a) the faithful on earth; (b) those in purgatory; (c) the saints in heaven; (d) b and c; (e) a, b, and c.

____ 3. We can pray for the souls in purgatory, but they cannot pray for us. (T or F)

____ 4. The dogma of the Immaculate Conception holds that Mary was always a virgin. (T or F)

____ 5. It is correct to say that Mary was the mother of the human Jesus; however, it is wrong to call her the Mother of God. (T or F)

There's a story about two little teardrops floating down the river of life. One teardrop curiously asked the other, "Who are you?"

"I am a teardrop from a beautiful girl who loved a guy and proceeded to lose him. But now I ask, who are you?"

"That's an easy question. I'm a teardrop from the unfortunate girl who got him."

Life is like this. So often we lament the things we cannot get, but we shed twice the tears if we receive them. Saint Paul taught that the source of our satisfaction is none other than Jesus, the Lord.

How would you describe your relationship with Jesus? With the Church?

KEY TERMS

Assumption of Mary

Blessed Ever Virgin

communion of saints

Immaculate Conception of Mary

Litany

Mary, Mother of God

Novena

Rosary

saints

Turning our lives over to Jesus is the key to sanctity. In this chapter, we will be looking at the communion of saints, that is, the Church as the union of all God's people. We will also study church teaching about Mary, the preeminent saint, our perfect model for holiness. She is the person who faithfully and totally surrendered herself to doing God's will through her Son.

(Catechism of the Catholic Church, 946–959)

Communion of Saints

It is like this with Christ's Body, the Church. We form one body in Christ, the Head; the good of each member is communicated and shared with others. This is especially true of Jesus Christ who shares his grace with all of us. In a family when something good happens to one, all members share in it. Similarly, in Christ's family, each member shares in the spiritual benefits of the others.

The term **communion of saints** refers to two realities: communion in holy things and communion among holy persons.

Holy Things

The "holy things" we share in common include our Christian faith and the graces of the sacraments, especially the Eucharist, which we so aptly call Holy Communion. We also share the benefits that result from our special gifts, or charisms; the material goods we share with each other, especially the needy, and our common work for justice. Moreover, we have a communion in charity (love), the great gift that is the spiritual glue that makes us one in Christ Jesus. Through the Eucharist the unity of believers is both represented and brought about. In solidarity with both

those alive and those who have departed this life, our smallest acts of loving kindness bring credit to the entire Body of Christ, the Church.

Holy Persons

The communion among "holy persons" includes the Pilgrim Church (on earth), the church suffering (in purgatory), and the church triumphant (in heaven). We believe that Christians— those living on earth and those who have gone to their eternal reward—are one family united in the Spirit of Christ Jesus. Just as members of a family depend on each other, so the members of God's family are interdependent.

Love is the spiritual energy that unites us. And prayer is a major and powerful

Consider for a few minutes seven different groups to which you belong. List them in the space provided. Then in the left column, list something this group gives you. Finally, in the right column, list something you give to the group. An example is provided.

Description of the Group

Example: band

    fun   **hard work**

I am primarily: ____ a giver
[check one]   ____ a taker
                      ____ pretty balanced in my relationships

List three things you could do in the next few weeks to contribute more generously to the members of a group to which you belong:

1.

2.

3.

way to stay in touch with our family members. We should never underestimate its power.

Those of us alive on earth depend on the prayers and good works of our Christian brothers and sisters who are one with us in the Lord's friendship. It is a valuable practice to pray for them and ask for their prayers and to offer our good works for their intentions. Our faith community also places great value on prayers for the dead who are suffering in purgatory. Our prayer can help them. Similarly, their prayers for us can be a great benefit for our earthly pilgrimage.

In a special way we believe the saints in heaven continue to pray for the church suffering and the church militant. They can also offer for our benefit the merits of their good works done on earth through Jesus Christ, our only Mediator and Savior.

The doctrine of the communion of saints highlights our interrelationship with the countless other members of Christ's family. We benefit from their prayers, goodness, and love for us, though we often do not perceive these connections. But life in Christ Jesus is communion. We are never alone.

The fervent prayer of a righteous person is very powerful.

James 5:16

The Saints

We belong to a community of saints. The Lord calls all of us to be holy, to live as children of God. Sanctity is not the vocation of a precious few. Christ gives everyone the many means to live a holy life. He gives us the grace and strength of the Holy Spirit, especially the gift of love, which is the supreme virtue to help us. Above all he gives us his very self in the Eucharist.

The saints—those Christian heroes who have gone before us and have shown us how to live the Christian life—are also another great help to us in living a holy life. The process of canonization, or naming a person a saint, involves a meticulous examination of the holy person's life. It also requires a sign from God, usually two miracles performed in that person's name. These help the Church discern that this person is a worthy guide for us and can serve as our intercessor. When the Church officially honors a saint, it is really praising God who has shared his holiness with us, both by giving us earthly models and heavenly friends.

There are countless saints in heaven who are not officially canonized. Many of these are our own relatives—for example, great grandparents, going back many generations. It is comforting to know that they are still connected to us in God's mysterious plan and that they pray for us and are concerned for us. We honor all these heroic, but often unknown, saints, on November 1, the feast of All Saints. Someday, we hope and pray, we will join them.

Devotion to the Saints

Catholics have always found devotion to the saints one important way to help us live holy lives. Devotion to saints includes veneration of them, not worship that is due God alone. We do not pray to the saints as though they were God Almighty. Rather, we ask them to intercede for us with our heavenly Father.

Devotion to the saints also includes learning about their lives and imitating one or another of their heroic virtues. For example, when Ignatius of Loyola (1491–1556) was recovering from a battle wound, he read the lives of the saints. What he read so moved him that he vowed to reform his life. He subsequently committed himself wholeheartedly to become a saint, a goal he achieved with distinction. We can relate to these flesh-and-blood people who proved their worth by rising to the challenge of the Christian life. This is especially true of the greatest saint of all—Mary, the Mother of God, and our Blessed Mother too.

> "**N**o devotion to the saints is more acceptable and proper than if you strive to express their virtue."
>
> &
>
> Erasmus

(CCC, 484–507, 963–972)

Mary, the Mother of Christ, Mother of the Church

Because of her special role in salvation history, Catholics revere Mary as the foremost saint. Her words "Let it be done according to your word" said yes to the incarnation of the Son of God. Her cooperation with God gave Mary a unique role in God's loving plan of goodness and salvation for all people.

Mary, Mother of Christ

The New Testament tells us that the young virgin Mary, not fully understanding how she was to conceive a child, became a perfect model of faith when she assented to Gabriel's news that she was to bear God's Son. Her Magnificat (Luke 1:46–55) reveals her to be a humble, gracious, and joyous model for us. She praised God for singling her out to be the mother of the savior. In humility, she accepted her role in God's plan. Her trust in his Word makes her the supreme model of faith and the most honorable of all Christians.

Mary devoted her whole life to Jesus. With Joseph, she raised him in a loving and caring home. She celebrated the Sabbath with him and accompanied him to Jerusalem for the major religious feasts. Mary supported Jesus during his public ministry and sorrowfully stood at the foot of the cross in his dying moments. She prayed with the apostles in the upper room after Jesus' ascension, awaiting the coming of the Holy Spirit.

These examples from the New Testament reveal Mary, the Mother of Christ, to be a model of Christian faith and love. In a singular way she cooperated with her son Jesus' redemptive work and always responded obediently to the promptings of the Holy Spirit.

Because of Mary's exemplary life and her unique role in salvation history, the Church honors her with the titles Mother of God and Mother of the

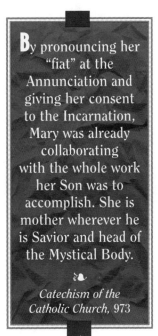

By pronouncing her "fiat" at the Annunciation and giving her consent to the Incarnation, Mary was already collaborating with the whole work her Son was to accomplish. She is mother wherever he is Savior and head of the Mystical Body.

Catechism of the Catholic Church, 973

Church. Other titles of Mary include Our Lady, Our Lady of the Immaculate Conception, Ever Virgin, and Queen of Heaven and Earth. A favorite name for Mary is, of course, the Blessed Mother. Each of these titles reflects an aspect of Catholic belief about Mary. Each honors her as the greatest of the saints.

The Church believes the following about Mary:

Immaculate Conception

The doctrine of the Immaculate Conception holds that Mary was conceived without original sin. This means that from the first moment of her existence, Mary was "full of grace," free from any alienation from God caused by original sin. We believe that because of the special role she was to have in salvation history, God graced Mary with this divine favor in anticipation of Christ's Paschal mystery. In addition, Mary lived a sinless life. When Gabriel proclaimed, "Hail, favored one! The Lord is with you" (Luke 1:28), he was heralding that Mary is the most blessed of all humans. Her role in salvation history is unique and central. She, God's Mother, is all-holy.

Mother of God

In chapter 3 we saw how, guided by the Holy Spirit, the early Church taught that Jesus is one divine person who has both a divine and a human nature. Further, the Church taught that, from the very first moment of his conception, Jesus was divine. The Council of Ephesus solemnly proclaimed that

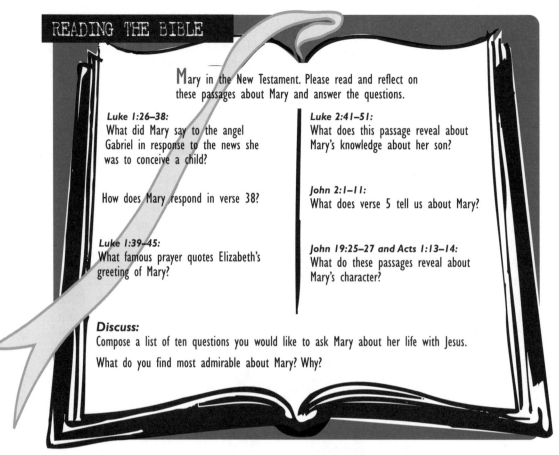

Mary in the New Testament. Please read and reflect on these passages about Mary and answer the questions.

Luke 1:26–38:
What did Mary say to the angel Gabriel in response to the news she was to conceive a child?

How does Mary respond in verse 38?

Luke 1:39–45:
What famous prayer quotes Elizabeth's greeting of Mary?

Luke 2:41–51:
What does this passage reveal about Mary's knowledge about her son?

John 2:1–11:
What does verse 5 tell us about Mary?

John 19:25–27 and Acts 1:13–14:
What do these passages reveal about Mary's character?

Discuss:
Compose a list of ten questions you would like to ask Mary about her life with Jesus.

What do you find most admirable about Mary? Why?

Mary is the "Mother of God" (in Greek, *Theo-tokos,* "God bearer") in A.D. 431. Because Mary is Christ's mother, it is true to say that she is truly the Mother of God.

Ever Virgin

The Apostles' Creed affirms that Jesus, conceived by the Holy Spirit, was born of the Virgin Mary. Jesus was conceived without a human father. The Church has traditionally taught that Mary was always a virgin, "before, in, and after" the birth of the Lord. We cannot fully understand this mystery. However, with the eyes of faith, we can discern its meaning. Beliefs about Mary find their roots in our faith about Jesus Christ. From all eternity, God chose Mary to be the mother of the Lord and Savior, Jesus Christ. As a true daughter of an Israelite, Mary was the last in the line

of holy women who cooperated in God's plan of salvation. In faith, she assented to Gabriel's announcement that she was to conceive a child. As a result, she helped God's plan to bear fruit. Mary's virginity highlights the truth that God took the initiative in the Incarnation. God the Father is the only Father of our Savior!

Mother of the Church

We also call Mary the Mother of the Church. When he hung dying on the cross, Jesus entrusted his mother to all of us to be our spiritual mother, saying, "Behold, your mother" (John 19:27). Mary is truly the new Eve, our mother whose obedience to the Holy Spirit helped bring Christ into the world.

Mary is above all else the loving Mother of our Savior and our Blessed Mother.

She continues to intercede for us today before her Son, just as she did for the couple who ran out of wine at the wedding feast of Cana. The Church recognizes this truth and so honors her with additional titles like Advocate, Helper, Benefactress, and Mediatrix.

As one of us, Mary also brings us to Christ. Her strong faith and unceasing love help give birth to new Christians who are called to resemble her fidelity and devotion. Mary gives us tremendous hope. She inspires us by showing what God does for his loved ones. She images God's love for his people and is a model of holiness.

Assumption

The doctrine of the Assumption, which has roots in ancient Catholic belief, links Mary's preservation from original sin and the mystery of our faith that we will be raised to new life with Christ Jesus. Pope Pius XII explained in 1950: "The Immaculate Mother of God, the ever Virgin Mary, having completed the course of her earthly life, was assumed body and soul into heavenly glory."

By her Assumption, the decay of death did not touch Mary. She, the Mother of God, is the first to share in her Son's resurrection. She serves as a special sign of hope for all of us striving for eternal union with the Risen Lord. Her Assumption, celebrated on August 15 as a holy day, anticipates our own final glory.

Devotion to Mary

One distinguishing characteristic of Catholicism is its devotion to the Blessed Mother. Our prayer to and honor of her helps us love her as our own mother. They also inspire us to imitate her obedience to God's will.

Sometimes Catholics are accused of "worshiping" Mary, of making her equal to God. This is a false charge. Mary is our mother whom we honor, but Jesus is our one and only Savior, the unique mediator between God and us. We worship God alone, but we venerate Mary as a uniquely blessed person who strongly attracts us to her Son. Her role in God's plan is to give Jesus to us. Her fidelity, gentleness, and loving care model how we should respond to him. Her motherly concern is undying as she prays for us "now and at the hour of our death."

Another popular devotion to Mary is the Angelus. This devotion commemorates the Incarnation and is typically recited in the morning, at the noon hour, and in the evening. The Angelus contains short biblical verses recalling the Annunciation, three Hail Marys, and a special prayer.

The First Saturday devotion resulted from Mary's appearances in 1917 to

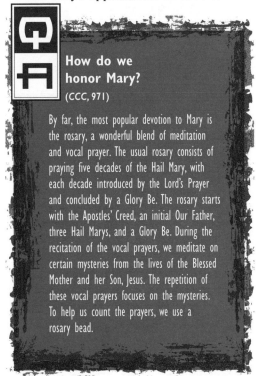

How do we honor Mary?
(CCC, 971)

By far, the most popular devotion to Mary is the rosary, a wonderful blend of meditation and vocal prayer. The usual rosary consists of praying five decades of the Hail Mary, with each decade introduced by the Lord's Prayer and concluded by a Glory Be. The rosary starts with the Apostles' Creed, an initial Our Father, three Hail Marys, and a Glory Be. During the recitation of the vocal prayers, we meditate on certain mysteries from the lives of the Blessed Mother and her Son, Jesus. The repetition of these vocal prayers focuses on the mysteries. To help us count the prayers, we use a rosary bead.

three children in Fatima, Portugal. It consists of going to confession, receiving Holy Communion on the first Saturday of five consecutive months, and reciting and meditating on the mysteries of the rosary. The practice is offered for the conversion of sinners and to repair the harm done caused by sin.

Other Marian devotions include the Litany of the Blessed Mother and various novenas. A **litany** is a series of prayers with responses. A **novena** is practiced over nine consecutive days or weeks to commemorate the period of prayer spent by Mary and the apostles in the upper room in Jerusalem before the Holy Spirit descended on Pentecost Sunday.

Magnificat

"My soul proclaims the greatness
   of the Lord;
   my spirit rejoices in God my savior.
For he has looked upon his
   handmaid's lowliness;
   behold, from now on will all ages
   call me blessed.
The Mighty One has done great things
   for me,
   and holy is his name.
His mercy is from age to age
   to those who fear him.
He has shown might with his arm,
   dispersed the arrogant of mind
   and heart.
He has thrown down the rulers from
   their thrones
   but lifted up the lowly.
The hungry he has filled with good
   things;
   the rich he has sent away empty.
He has helped Israel his servant,
   remembering his mercy,
according to his promise to our fathers,
   to Abraham and to his
   descendants forever."

Luke 1:46–55

REVIEW

IMPORTANT TERMS TO KNOW

Assumption of Mary—Proclaimed in 1950 by Pope Pius XII, this church dogma holds that the Blessed Mother, when her earthly life was finished, was taken directly to heaven. We celebrate the Feast of the Assumption on August 15, a holy day of obligation.

Blessed Ever Virgin—title for Mary that expresses our belief in Mary's real and perpetual virginity even in the act of Mary's giving birth to Jesus; Jesus was conceived solely by the power of the Holy Spirit; Mary was a virgin before, during, and after the conception and birth of Jesus

communion of saints—The entire Mystical Body of Christ—those on earth, in purgatory, and in heaven—and their spiritual union in grace, prayer, and good works

Immaculate Conception of Mary—The church dogma that holds that the Blessed Mother was free from sin from the very first moment of her human existence. We celebrate this feast on December 8, a holy day of obligation. (The Immaculate Conception is often confused with the doctrine of the virginal conception, which teaches that the Virgin Mary conceived Jesus by the power of the Holy Spirit without the cooperation of a human father.)

litany—A prayer form which includes fixed responses (for example, "Pray for Us") to a series of petitions. Two popular examples are the Litany to the Blessed Mother and the Litany of the Saints.

Mary, Mother of God—title of Mary that expresses our belief that Mary, the Mother of Christ, the Son of God become man is truly the Mother of God

novena—A public or private prayer devotion that extends over nine successive days or weeks. Various novenas to the Blessed Mother have been popular in the Church for centuries.

rosary—devotion to Mary that dates from the sixteenth century by which the faithful meditate on some aspect of the life of Christ or Mary

saints—those officially recognized by the Church as having lived holy lives, share in the life of heaven, and can be publically venerated by the faithful

CHAPTER SUMMARY

The Blessed Mother gave Jesus to the world. As her spiritual children, we are called to imitate her by taking him to others, especially by serving those in need. In this chapter we learned:

1. The Church is a "communion of saints." The communion of saints includes those alive on earth, the suffering in purgatory, and the blessed ones in heaven.

2. Christ calls all members of his family to sainthood. Canonized saints have lived heroic lives of Christian witness. We honor them by praying to them and by imitating their virtues.

3. The Church honors Mary as the most blessed human being. Mary is the Mother of God. Because Jesus entrusted her to us,

she is also our Blessed Mother. As the Mother of the Church, she constantly prays for us. We should pray to her often, using devotions like the rosary and her special prayer, the Hail Mary.

4. The doctrine of the Immaculate Conception teaches that Mary was free from sin from the very moment of her conception. The doctrine of Mary Ever Virgin holds that Mary remained a virgin before, during, and after the conception of Jesus. Mary's Assumption into heaven holds that when her earthly life was over, her body and soul were assumed into heaven. Because of her unique role in salvation history, Mary is the first to share in the glory of her Son's resurrection.

EXPLORING OUR CATHOLIC FAITH

1. Listening to God's Word

The Magnificat, Mary's great canticle of thanksgiving and praise of God, is found in Luke 1:46–55. Read and reflect on Mary's words. What does the Magnificat tell you about Mary? What does it reveal to you about who we are the spiritual children of Mary?

2. Understanding the Teachings of the Catholic Church

The bishops at the Second Vatican Council taught: "[Mary] is hailed as pre-eminent and as a wholly unique member of the Church, and as its type and outstanding model in faith and charity. . . . The Catholic Church taught by the Holy Spirit, honors her with filial affection and devotion as a most beloved mother" (*Dogmatic Constitution*

on the Church, 53). How do you see the Church living this teaching?

3. Reflecting on Our Catholic Faith

Reflect on this insight: "The Christian's life is the world's Bible."

What do others learn about God from your words and deeds? Write your thoughts in your journal.

4. Living Our Catholic Faith

We believe that we are a communion of saints. We are one family united in the Spirit of Christ Jesus. And just as members of a family support one another, so the members of God's family support one another. List the things you do that "show" that you are living that belief. What two things could you add to that list that you could do with others?

CHAPTER 10
Life Everlasting

"I am the resurrection and the life;
whoever believes in me, even if he dies, will live,
and everyone who lives and believes in me
will never die. Do you believe this?"

JOHN 11:25–26

A cemetery in a Midwestern state had a century-old tombstone with this epitaph engraved on it:

> Pause, Stranger, when you pass me by,
> As you are now, so once was I.
> As I am now, so you will be,
> So prepare for death and follow me.

An unknown passerby had read these words and was not quite satisfied with them. He scratched this reply:

> To follow you I'm not content,
> Until I know which way you went.

What a wise reply to a wise warning. We should always be prepared for death. But the important thing about death is what follows. The key question is, Where are you going?

Saint Bernard of Clairvaux wrote, "Death is the gate of life." What do these words tell us about the Church's belief about human life—and death?

KEY TERMS

beatific vision

eschatology

judgment

heaven

hell

kingdom of God

purgatory

resurrection of the body

The Apostles' Creed links faith in the forgiveness of sins with faith in the Holy Spirit, faith in the Church, and faith in the communion of saints. We pray:

> I believe in . . . the forgiveness of sins, the resurrection of the body, and the life everlasting.

If our sins are forgiven, we do not have to fear death or judgment. If we die in the friendship of Jesus, we will be raised to eternal glory with him.

This chapter will treat topics in the area of **eschatology.** Eschatology is the branch of theology that studies the "last things"—death, judgment, heaven, hell, purgatory, the resurrection of the body, the second coming of Christ, and life everlasting.

(*Catechism of the Catholic Church*, 976–983)

The Forgiveness of Sins

In the account of Jesus' birth in Matthew's Gospel, we read:

[T]he angel of the Lord appeared to [Joseph] in a dream and said, . . . "[Mary] will bear a son and you are to name him Jesus, because he will save his people from their sins."

Matthew 1:20–21

Baptism

Forgiveness of sins was at the heart of Jesus' earthly ministry. Ever since that birthday of the Church, new Christians have received baptism and adoption into God's family. A major effect of baptism is the complete forgiveness of both original sin and one's personal offenses. Baptism is the primary sacrament of forgiveness because it wipes away sin and unites us to Christ Jesus.

Sin and the Sacrament of Penance

Though baptism does indeed forgive our sins, the grace of baptism does not free us from the weakness of human nature and our inclination to sin. Unfortunately, we do sin after baptism. Some of this sin can be deadly, or mortal. Committed with freedom and knowledge, mortal sin "kills" our relationship with God and alienates us from the members of God's family and even ourselves.

Many have observed that people don't go to confession as much today as in previous generations. Why do you think this is so? What place does the "forgiveness of sins" play in your life?

Discuss your responses with the members of your group.

Sin is a turning of our backs on God and the community of the Church. When we sin, we need to be "reconciled with God and the Church." We need to convert once again and renounce our sin sincerely and contritely. We are contrite when we are truly sorry for our sins. We show true sorrow when we sincerely intend to avoid sin and what leads us into sin and repair any harm our sins have caused.

Power of the Keys

Christ died for all people so that we could be healed of our sins, be reborn as adopted children of God, and be reconciled with God and one another. We believe that the Lord, before his resurrection, handed over to the apostles the power to forgive sins committed after baptism.

The Lord left with the apostles and their successors the "power of the keys," that is, the authority to forgive postbaptismal sin in his name.

> [H]e breathed on them and said to them, "Receive the holy Spirit. Whose sins you forgive are forgiven them, and whose sins you retain are retained."
> **John 20:22–23**

This power to forgive sins—no matter how serious—continues in the Church today through bishops and priests.

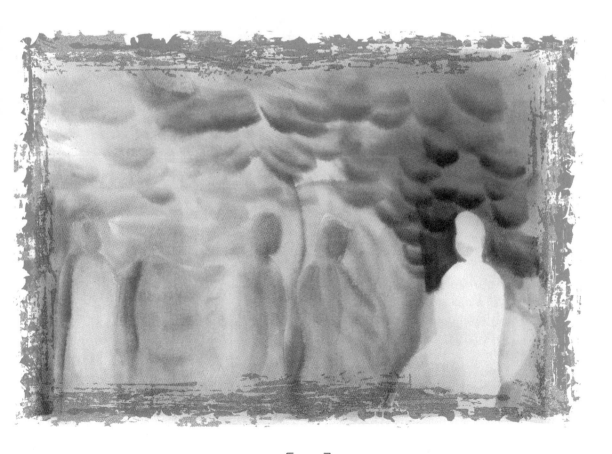

Christian Death and the Resurrection of the Body

Recall what Saint Bernard of Clairvaux wrote about death: "Death is the gate of life." We believe that:

❑ death is the end of earthly life;

❑ death is a consequence of sin;

❑ death is transformed by Christ.

Death, defined as the separation of the eternal soul from the body, is a great mystery. Though we consider death a natural phenomenon, we believe that death is a consequence of sin and that God did not originally intend humans to submit to death. Had Adam and Eve not turned from God, the human race would be immune from death as we know it.

Most importantly, we believe that Jesus Christ has conquered death. As a man, Jesus' impending death caused him great anguish. But by placing his trust in his Father, Jesus' death on the cross transformed death's curse into a great blessing.

By his own death and resurrection, the Lord has overcome our death and won salvation for all people. We give thanks and praise to God, saying:

Lord, for your faithful people life is changed, not ended. When the body of our earthly dwelling lies in death we gain an everlasting dwelling place in heaven.

Roman Missal,
Preface, Christian Death I

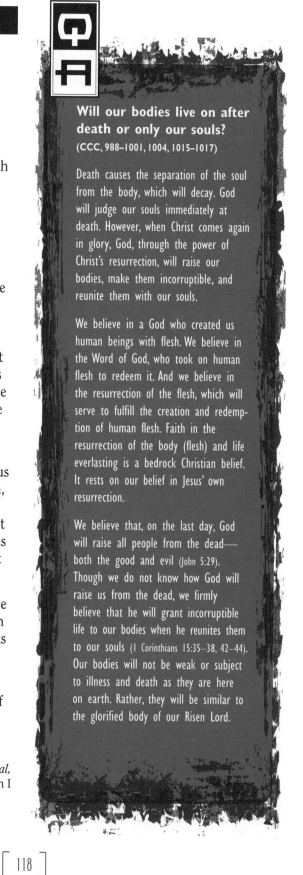

Will our bodies live on after death or only our souls?
(CCC, 988–1001, 1004, 1015–1017)

Death causes the separation of the soul from the body, which will decay. God will judge our souls immediately at death. However, when Christ comes again in glory, God, through the power of Christ's resurrection, will raise our bodies, make them incorruptible, and reunite them with our souls.

We believe in a God who created us human beings with flesh. We believe in the Word of God, who took on human flesh to redeem it. And we believe in the resurrection of the flesh, which will serve to fulfill the creation and redemption of human flesh. Faith in the resurrection of the body (flesh) and life everlasting is a bedrock Christian belief. It rests on our belief in Jesus' own resurrection.

We believe that, on the last day, God will raise all people from the dead—both the good and evil (John 5:29). Though we do not know how God will raise us from the dead, we firmly believe that he will grant incorruptible life to our bodies when he reunites them to our souls (1 Corinthians 15:35–38, 42–44). Our bodies will not be weak or subject to illness and death as they are here on earth. Rather, they will be similar to the glorified body of our Risen Lord.

Our Lord's Paschal mystery has revealed that death is not simply an end to our existence. It is our birthday into an eternal life of union with our loving God. We believe that
"If we have died with him
we shall also live with him"
(2 Timothy 2:11).
Just as Christ is risen and lives forever, so all of us will rise on the last day.

Deep down, we fear death. This fear is perfectly natural. However, our faith in the death and resurrection of Christ helps us cope with that fear and realize that "death is the gate of life." We place our faith and hope in Jesus, who promised:

"I am the resurrection and the life; whoever believes in me, even if he dies, will live, and everyone who lives and believes in me will never die. Do you believe this?"

John 11:25–26

We believe that Jesus Christ is our resurrection and our life. Made one with him in baptism, he is the source of our eternal life with God, with the Holy Trinity, with Mary and all the saints.

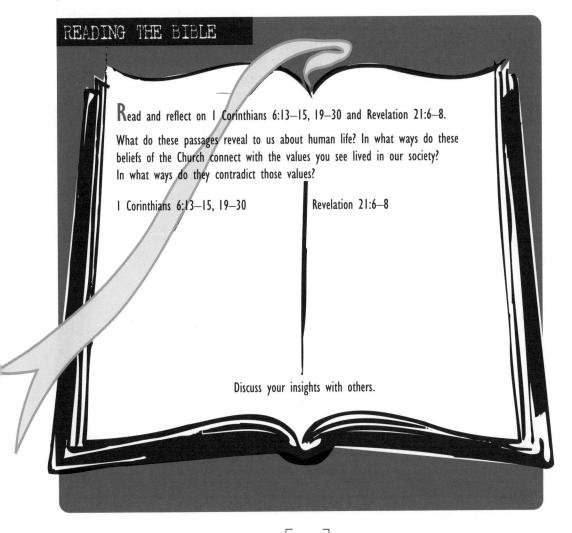

READING THE BIBLE

Read and reflect on 1 Corinthians 6:13–15, 19–30 and Revelation 21:6–8.

What do these passages reveal to us about human life? In what ways do these beliefs of the Church connect with the values you see lived in our society? In what ways do they contradict those values?

1 Corinthians 6:13–15, 19–30

Revelation 21:6–8

Discuss your insights with others.

Particular Judgment, Heaven, Purgatory, Hell

The Bible makes it clear that there will be a judgment after death. Paul writes:

> For we must all appear before the judgment seat of Christ, so that each one may receive recompense, according to what he did in the body, whether good or evil.
>
> **2 Corinthians 5:10**

Immediately after death each person will appear before God for a particular, or individual, judgment. Jesus taught about the particular judgment in the parable of the rich man and Lazarus (Luke 16:19–31). In the parable the selfish rich man refused to feed the poor and hungry Lazarus. For the rich man the payoff in the afterlife was the eternal suffering in the netherworld, or hell. Lazarus, on the other hand, was "carried away by angels to the bosom of Abraham," or to an eternal, peaceful resting place.

If we die in union with Christ, we do not need to fear God's judgment after we cross the threshold into eternal life. God is just and merciful. The Lord's judgment will be a just declaration of what we are—how we have loved him or not, how we have loved other people because of him or not (Matthew 25:31–46). This judgment will declare us ready for entering into heaven, either immediately or after purification in purgatory, or into hell and eternal suffering.

READING THE BIBLE

Judgment. The New Testament has many interesting things to say about judgment. Read John 5 and answer these questions.

Why was Jesus being persecuted (John 5:16)?

What authority does the Son have (John 5:22)?

Why did his opponents want to kill Jesus (John 5:18)?

What is the basis for eternal life (John 5:23)?

Heaven

If we die in God's friendship and grace, we will live forever in communion with the Holy Trinity, our Blessed Mother, and all the angels and saints. We will enjoy the **beatific vision,** that is, we will see God face-to-face, as he really is, contemplating his heavenly glory.

Heaven is the state of supreme happiness and a blessed and loving communion with God and God's creatures. In heaven we will be fully incorporated into Christ and will reign with Christ Jesus forever. The pleasures and happiness in store for us in heaven are beyond human imagination.

> "What eye has not seen,
> and ear has not heard,
> and what has not entered the
> human heart,
> what God has prepared for
> those who love him."
> **I Corinthians 2:9**

Purgatory

Catholics believe in the doctrine of **purgatory.** We believe that those who die in God's grace and friendship but who still need purification or cleansing of their venial sins or any punishment due sins that remain at death have the opportunity to achieve the holiness necessary to enjoy eternal happiness.

Purgatory involves a paradox. On the one hand, those in purgatory are joyful and happy because the Lord has guaranteed them the gift of eternal happiness. However, those "being purified" still need to let go of all their selfish attachments before embracing the all-holy God. This surrendering of selfish attachments involves some pain, which is described as the "fires of purgatory."

Perhaps the souls in purgatory "burn" with sorrow over their sins, as they longingly desire to be with the all-good God who has saved them. This separation from the One they desire to love so deeply—a separation caused by their own hesitations to love—causes suffering.

As members of the communion of saints, we should remember to pray for those in purgatory. A great way to honor our deceased relatives is to pray and offer sacrifices for them. They will be

Discuss

Scripture uses images to help describe heaven; for example, wedding feast, light, life, peace, paradise, the Father's house, heavenly Jerusalem.

What do these say to you about heaven?

If you were explaining our Catholic belief about heaven to a nonbeliever, what image would you use? Why?

sure to remember us in a special way when they finally meet our loving God face-to-face in heaven.

Hell

Hell is eternal death, eternal separation from God, who loves us and who created us for a life of everlasting joy and happiness. Scripture and Tradition both affirm the existence of hell. In his teaching about the destination of those who refuse to respond to the needs of the needy and the helpless ones, Jesus taught:

> "Then he will say to those on his left, 'Depart from me, you accursed, into the eternal fire prepared for the devil and his angels. . . . 'Amen, I say to you, what you did not do for one of these least ones, you did not do for me.'"
>
> **Matthew 25:41, 45**

"Hell fire" is an apt image for love lost. It describes well those who "burn" with self-hatred and abject loneliness because they have chosen self over a loving God and other people.

The pains of hell include grief over eternal punishment, spiritual and physical anguish, and despair of salvation. If we freely refuse to love God and others by deliberately committing mortal sin and die unrepentant, we will forever remain separated from God and the angels and saints by our own free choice. God forever showers his love on us; his mercy is always there for us to embrace. Nevertheless, a person can be hardhearted and stiffnecked, adamantly selfish and unloving.

The sincere Christian should not be unduly frightened of hell. If we are sincerely trying to love God and others as ourselves, we trust and believe that we will live forever with Christ as he promised. And if we sin, we trust that God will always forgive us when we turn to him with a contrite heart.

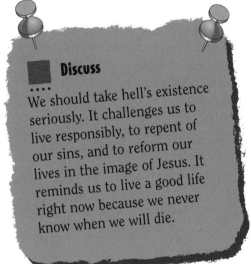

Discuss

We should take hell's existence seriously. It challenges us to live responsibly, to repent of our sins, and to reform our lives in the image of Jesus. It reminds us to live a good life right now because we never know when we will die.

(CCC, 1038–1065)

The Last, or General, Judgment

Christians believe that at the end of time the kingdom of God will come in its fullness and the just will reign with Christ forever.

The Last Judgment

On that final day, the Lord will come again in all his glory and all—the just and the unjust—will appear before the Lord in their bodies. The Lord and Judge will then reveal each person's relationship with God, and everyone will recognize God's saving plan in

Christ Jesus. As to when this will take place, only the Father knows.

The New Testament gives a vivid picture of this day.

> "When the Son of Man comes in his glory, and all the angels with him, he will sit upon his glorious throne, and all the nations will be assembled before him. And he will separate them one from another, as a shepherd separates the sheep from the goats."
>
> **Matthew 25:31–32**

New Heavens and New Earth

On that promised day, Christ's goodness, mercy, justice, and peace will usher in the kingdom, or reign, of God in all its glory. Everyone will marvel at and acknowledge the Lord's majesty and kingship. Christians look forward to the Second Coming because Christ will then bring about the final unity of the human race. On this glorious day, God will transform the physical universe. He will restore it to its original state so it can share in the glory of Christ Jesus.

Because Jesus has already inaugurated God's reign, even today we have a foretaste of the future. We believe God's loving grace is saving people right now.

Many forces in today's world oppose God's love and his plan for the salvation of all. However, the Holy Spirit gives us many gifts to work toward building that kingdom. Fortitude, for example, strengthens us to help the Lord establish his reign of justice and peace. Hope enables us to look forward to the day when God's kingdom will be fully established.

WHAT THE DOCUMENTS SAY

We are taught that God is preparing a new dwelling and a new earth in which righteousness dwells.

Pastoral Constitution on the Church in the Modern World, 39

Imagine what the "new dwelling" and "new earth" might be like. How can you work toward it?

Amen

Both the Apostles' Creed and the Bible conclude with the Hebrew word *Amen*. *Amen* means "so be it," "I agree," "certainly," "it is firm." The root of *Amen* in Hebrew means "believe." When we say "Amen," we are making an act of faith. We are proclaiming the truth of what has just preceded this response.

In a very real sense, Jesus himself is God's "Amen." He is the "Yes" of the Father's love for us. Our Lord used "Amen" frequently to emphasize the trustworthiness of his teaching—to emphasize that its origin is in God.

In a certain sense, Christian death is an "Amen" that punctuates the story of a Christian's life. It is a statement of belief-put-into-action that we take to God for his loving embrace when our life's journey is over.

Alpha and Omega

"I [am] the Alpha and the Omega, the beginning and the end. To the thirsty I will give a gift from the spring of life-giving water." Revelation 21:6

Alpha (A) is the first letter of the Greek alphabet; omega is the last. The Book of Revelation refers to Jesus, the Judge, as the Alpha and the Omega (Revelation 1:8). He is the beginning and the end. He will come at the end of time to judge the living and the dead.

REVIEW

IMPORTANT TERMS TO KNOW

beatific vision—the happiness of seeing God face-to-face in heaven that results from final union with the Triune God for all eternity

eschatology—the branch of theology that studies the "last things"—death, judgment, heaven, hell, purgatory, the Second Coming, the resurrection of the body, and life everlasting

judgment—the determination of one's destiny. The general judgment is Jesus' judgment of the living and the dead at the end of time when he will come to establish the kingdom of God fully; the particular judgment takes place immediately after death and determines one's eternal destiny in heaven (after purification in purgatory, if needed) or hell.

heaven—eternal happiness and life with God and the communion of saints for all eternity. It is the state of supreme, definitive happiness that human hearts deeply desire.

hell—eternal death and separation from God brought on by a person who dies with unrepented mortal sin. Hell results from a person's free and deliberate choice to thwart God's will.

kingdom of God—the image or symbol used in Scripture that describes the living of all people and creation in communion with God. The kingdom will come about when Christ comes again in glory.

purgatory—the state or condition of purification after death for those who die in God's friendship yet still need to be purified to attain holiness before entering heaven

resurrection of the body—the teaching that at the general judgment the Lord will unite the soul of every person who ever lived to its own body. The Lord will also glorify the bodies of those destined for heaven.

CHAPTER SUMMARY

In this final chapter of the book, we have been studying Christian eschatology—church teaching on death, resurrection, judgment, heaven, purgatory, and hell. We learned that:

1. Christ gave to the apostles and their successors his power to forgive sin in his name. Baptism wipes away all sin. If a person sincerely and contritely confesses postbaptismal sin in the sacrament of confession, sin is forgiven.

2. Death as we know it was not part of God's original plan for us. Death was introduced by Adam's sin. Christ Jesus overcame death by his own sacrifice on the cross and resurrection. If we die in Christ, we will rise on the last day to share in the Lord's glory. The resurrection of the dead means our bodies will rise to an incorruptible, eternal life joined to our souls.

3. At the moment of death, each person will appear before God for a particular judgment.

This individual judgment will decide if we enter heaven, purgatory, or hell.

4. Heaven is eternal union with God, where the just will possess the beatific vision. Purgatory is the state of purification for those who die in God's friendship but need cleansing to achieve the holiness necessary to see the all-holy God. Hell is eternal death and eternal separation from God brought on by a person who dies in unrepented mortal sin.

5. At the end of time, there will be a general judgment of the just and unjust. On that day all will appear before Christ in their own bodies to render an account of their own deeds.

6. At the end of time, the kingdom of God will come in its fullness. Then the just will reign with Christ forever. God will be "all in all." Christ will unify the human race and transform the physical universe to share in his glory.

EXPLORING OUR CATHOLIC FAITH

1. Listening to God's Word

Read John 11:25–26 and Revelation 21:4 and quietly listen to the Word God speaks to us. What is God's promise to us? How does that promise motivate you to live?

2. Understanding the Teachings of the Catholic Church

The prayers of the Church's liturgy both celebrate and profess our faith. When we gather to celebrate the funeral Mass, the presider leads us in prayer, saying:

> By your power you bring us to birth.
> By your providence you rule our lives.
> By your command you free us at last from sin
> as we return to the dust from which we came.
> Through the saving death of your Son
> we rise at your word to the glory of the
> resurrection.

What does this prayer "teach" about our Catholic faith? How does it help us "celebrate" our death?

3. Reflecting on Our Catholic Faith

Reflect on this insight: "There are only War Veterans in heaven, who have fought the good fight for the Kingdom of God" (Archbishop Fulton J. Sheen, *The Fullness of Christ*, 1935). How does this insight help you keep focused on your journey of faith? Write your thoughts in your journal.

4. Living Our Catholic Faith

We can and must cooperate with Christ's work of liberation. We help the Lord in his work by becoming peacemakers and by helping people attain their God-given rights. We also cooperate in Christ's plan when we promote human solidarity and respect the dignity of every human being. In a special way, we promote the kingdom of God when we extend mercy to the weak, poor, and defenseless.

Index

M

Magisterium of Church
    definition of, 16
    infallibility of, 87
    role of, in Church, 14
Magnificat, 109, 112
marks of Church, 94–101
    apostolic, 100–101
    catholic, 98–100
    holy, 96–98
    one, 94–96
Mary, 108–112
    Assumption of, 111
    devotion to, 111–12
    as greatest saint, 98
    Immaculate Conception of, 37, 112
    as Mother of Christ, 109–11
    as Mother of Church, 110–11
    as Mother of God, 37, 109–110, 112
    virginity of, 37, 110
miracles of Jesus, 39
missions of the Holy Trinity, 75–76
Monophysitism, 39
Moses, 12
mystery, meaning of, 80, 90
Mystical Body of Christ, 81

N

Nestorianism, 39
New Testament
    nature of, 13
    writings in, 32–35
Nicene Creed, 15–16
novena, 112

O

Old Testament,
    nature of, 13
    writings in, 21–23
original sin, 26–28
Orthodox churches, 100

P-Q

Paschal mystery
    Father and, 70–71
    Holy Spirit and, 60
    human death and, 119
    meaning of, 39–40, 44
Penance, sacrament of, 116–17
Pentateuch, 21
Pentecost, 56–57, 69
People of God, Church as, 82–83
Pilgrim Church, 106
pope
    ministry of, 86–87
    as successor of apostle Peter, 101
Power of the Keys, 117
priest(s)
    ministry of, 87
prophets,
    role of, in salvation history, 12
    writings of, 22

Protestant churches, relationship of, to Catholic
        Church, 100
providence. *See* divine providence.
purgatory, 106–107, 121–22, 124

R

religious life, 86
resurrection of body, 118–119, 124
Resurrection of Jesus, 49–51, 119
Revelation, New Testament Book of
revelation. *See* Divine Revelation.
rosary, 111, 112

S

sacrament
    definition of, 90
    presence of Risen Lord with Church
        through, 51
Sacred Scripture, 20–23
    canon of, 21
    definition of, 16
    inspiration of, 13, 20–21
    as source of divine revelation, 13
Sacred Tradition
    role of, in Church, 14
saint(s)
    canonization of, 98
    definition of, 112
    devotion to, 108
    See also communion of saints.
salvation
    fullness of, in Catholic Church, 94–95
    meaning of, 47–48
salvation history, 11
    Holy Spirit in, 61, 63–64
Satan, existence of, 26
schism, 94
secularism, 8
Sign of the Cross, 72
sin(s)
    forgiveness of, 60, 116–118
    original, 26–28
Son of God, 36, 46. *See also* Jesus Christ
Son of Man, 36
spirit, meaning of word, 58.
Spirit. *See* Holy Spirit.
Suffering Servant, 36, 48

T-U

Temple of Holy Spirit
    Church as, 47, 60, 85, 96, 101
Temptation of Jesus, 38
Tradition. *See* Sacred Tradition.
Transfiguration of Jesus, 39
Trinity. *See* Holy Trinity.

V-W

veneration of saints, 108
Word of God, 36

X-Z

Yahweh, 20, 28